The
BEGINNER'S GUIDE
to UPHOLSTERY

The
BEGINNER'S GUIDE
to UPHOLSTERY

10 achievable DIY upholstery and
reupholstery projects for your home

Vicky Grubb

DAVID & CHARLES

www.davidandcharles.com

CONTENTS

PROJECTS   22

TECHNIQUES

INTRODUCTION

Upholstery was not my initial choice of career. After university, I worked in research, which involved a great deal of travelling. I felt unfulfilled and after a visit to a career coach, I started to rediscover my creative roots. From the very first night class I took, I fell instantly in love with everything upholstery, and with the encouragement of my teacher, Sarah, and the support of an understanding employer, I enrolled for a one-day-a-week upholstery diploma course.

After successfully finishing my course, I took commissions via word of mouth, and through friends of friends, I received my first hotel contract. Although I dreamed of a fancy workshop, these starting-out commissions were all achieved on my kitchen table. Eventually I spent some time (and a little bit of money) converting our brick garage into my very own creative space, filling it with vintage fabrics, an oversized table made from old scaffold boards, and a 1930s kitchen cupboard full of threads and tools. At The Upholstery Studio, I take commissions, run upholstery courses and create my own furniture too, in between looking after two small children.

Kitchen Table Upholstery

All the projects in this book can be achieved from your kitchen table, so you don't have to think about renting a space just yet! After all, that was how I started: I kept my staples and tools in a handy tool bag and used plastic tubs to store my threads and needles in. As long as you have a system for your bits and bobs, there's no reason why you can't clear the plates from dinner, pop on the radio and upholster into the evening. My advice on a basic toolkit and tips on sourcing furniture and fabrics will set you on your way to upholstering your first project.

Keeping It Simple

There are numerous ways to upholster a chair with a variety of stuffing and fillings, and with the many tools and materials available, it can be a little daunting. But just as easily as you can whizz up a pair of bedroom curtains, you can make a headboard for your bed or cover a blanket box. In this book I take you through ten achievable projects that are ideal starter pieces for the fulfilling craft of upholstery. Using my step-by-step instructions and watching my online time-lapse videos to help you, you can learn how to upholster using modern upholstery techniques.

Happy Upholstering

Let your upholstery journey start here. I hope this guide gives you the confidence to go out and find furniture, spruce it up and give it a new place in your home. One of the things I most enjoy about upholstery is seeing my students' creations and I would love to see your transformations too. Here's how to get in touch with me:

email: vicky@somethingfine.co.uk
twitter: @something_fine
instagram: @something_fine
hashtag: #kitchentableupholstery

SOURCING FURNITURE

I love nothing more than an early morning mooch around a flea market. There is no telling what treasures I will find. I buy furniture online too and I love to pick up a bargain at a second-hand store. I want to share with you my tips of what to look for, and what to watch out for, when purchasing second-hand furniture.

A Modern Approach

I adore mid-century furniture and I've tried to keep things simple by using modern post-war furniture in this book. Antique furniture is upholstered using traditional upholstery techniques employing sophisticated stitching and is much more labour intensive. If you prefer antique-style furniture, you will find that most reproduction antique furniture is, and can be, upholstered using modern upholstery techniques.

Do Your Research

It's a good idea to try to pin down the furniture styles you like and the main manufacturers. Knowing the manufacturer will help you to gain knowledge of how their furniture pieces are constructed. A simple Google Images search or scour on Pinterest can give you numerous ways in which that particular frame has been upholstered.

You can use the Internet to search for an era or style of furniture you like: if you type in '1970s chair', for example, this will bring up lots of different styles and you can start to whittle it down to a specific type of dining or arm chair, say, and this, in turn, could be used to search for an exact item in an online auction site.

Tip

If you find a name on a furniture frame that you don't recognize, use your smart phone to look it up.

Where to Buy

There are several places I source furniture from:

- Local buy and sell sites
- National auction sites, such as eBay
- Flea markets
- Second-hand stores
- Vintage market warehouses

Each source has its merits and disadvantages. The cost of transporting the furniture is one of my biggest considerations. I have found the key to finding the right piece at the right time is searching regularly.

Vide greniers (France), car boot sales (UK) or garage sales (US) – the name may differ but all sell second-hand items for a fraction of what they would cost to buy new.

Think About Your Space

I always keep a tape measure in my handbag for any furniture sourcing misson. Getting a piece into the car is one thing, but it's also important to think about where you want to put it when you get it home. If I want to fit the item into a specific place, I make sure I type the measurements into my phone before I leave.

Buying Tips

I've compiled a list of things to look out for when out shopping for your perfect piece.

Wobbles and Creaks

Wobbly legs are fairly easy to fix, sometimes with an extra screw, or by using wood glue and a clamp. If the frame is creaking from side to side keep looking – the additional work may require a carpenter at more cost.

Spring Construction

Tying in springs to a chair can be a tricky business. For ease, look out for furniture constructed with spring mesh units, tension springs, rubber webbing or serpentine springs. Take a peek though the platform cloth or under the foam cushion. If it's a spring mesh unit, you'll be able to see the mesh sitting on the top of the coil spring. Even if the rubber or tension springs are past their best, they are easy to replace.

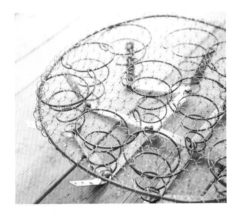

A spring mesh unit.

Tension springs on the back of a wing chair.

Age of Chair

Age is definitely not a bad thing when it comes to upholstery: older chairs tend to have much better frame construction and are designed to last, particularly if made from hardwood. However, unless you find a well-known manufacturer, it's not always obvious how the frame will be constructed. In this book I've included furniture made from plywood, hardwood and chipboard, but you may also find plastic and metal. Again, looking under the chair and peeking through the platform cloth can reveal a lot about the frame.

Appearance of Wood

Avoid chairs with substantial mould residue and lots of small holes in them caused by woodworm. Although both are treatable, it's difficult to know what permanent damage has been inflicted to the frame without stripping it back.

Caked-on Varnish

Removing varnish with paint stripper and wire wool takes a lot of hard work, so unless you like vigorous exercise avoid furniture with a lot of wood showing if luminous orange or the like.

Expect the Unexpected

After checking the springs and sizing it up, purchasing it at the best price and lugging it back home, what will you find beneath the layers of your furniture piece? There may be several layers of fabric with staples to remove before you even get to the stuffing, which may turn out to be straw; or a seemingly normal cushion might reveal itself to be filled with deteriorated crumbs, once a solid piece of foam. Don't worry – when your piece of furniture is stripped back to the frame, you can start to re-assemble it with my help.

FABRIC ESSENTIALS

I'm a self-confessed vintage fabric hoarder. I've been collecting for many years: it started small, just filling a blanket box, then it gradually grew. Now I have an enormous 1950s school cupboard stacked three deep with patterns, velvets and wools of all shades, some for upholstery, some for crafting and some just for the collection. Whether you buy vintage or new for your furniture upholstery projects is a personal choice but I hope my tips on where to buy and what to look out for will be useful.

Buying New Fabric

There are so many fabric designs available, it can be difficult to know where to start. I have a large box of samples I show to students and clients. Samples are really easy to get hold of and most companies will only charge you for the postage. To help you choose your ideal fabric, follow my tips and apply my four-step process to choosing fabric.

Pattern Size and Repeat

It's best to use smaller patterns for smaller furniture; however, a smaller pattern can look great on a large chair and a large pattern motif could be centred in a dining chair seat to great effect. The only way to find out is to order a sample.

When upholstering with patterned fabric there are a couple of things to take into account: first, you must allow for the pattern repeat in your fabric calculations as additional fabric is likely to be required, particularly if you are using a bold pattern (see Techniques: Measuring and Cutting Fabric); second, a little more precision is needed when matching the fabric around the chair, as you have to make sure that everything lines up properly.

My Four-Step Process to Choosing Fabric

Step One Head to your nearest fabric store to look at the fabric rolls and ask the assistant to recommend look books.

Step Two Use your phone to take photos of the fabrics you like. Take a front image to show the design and a back image for details on usage and manufacturer.

Step Three Armed with your fabric details, return home to do an internet search to see how people have used them and to find similar styles.

Step Four Order samples of your chosen fabric and place them on your furniture piece to check the scale.

When I assess a fabric sample, I check the edges to see if it frays too easily and I also stretch it in my hand to see if there is a little give.

Rub Count

Upholstery fabric is measured in rub counts (often written as Martindale test): the fabric is rubbed on a Martindale machine; the higher the number of rubs, the tougher the fabric. Generally the rub count will be identified in the fabric description, but if not, there should be some indication of what the fabric is suitable for, such as occasional use, light domestic, heavy domestic, light contract or heavy contract. If you are upholstering a chair that has a lot of use, you should choose a fabric that is a little tougher.

Fibre Content

Most upholstery fabrics fall into the following eight groups:

- Animal skins
- Coated fabrics, such as vinyl
- Knitted fabrics, such as jersey
- Non-woven fabrics, such as stitch or spun bonded
- Pile fabrics, such as velvet or corduroy
- Printed fabrics
- Woven plain fabrics, such as tweed or calico
- Woven patterned fabrics, such as damask or brocade

Most fabric labels will list the fabric composition. You may start to get a feel for the sort of fabrics you like just by looking and touching. Of course, there may be an important reason to look up fabric content, for ease of stain removal (low absorbency), or to avoid allergies (untreated) for example.

The Martindale Test

This is a rub test on fabrics, scored in 1000s of rubs. The higher the number is, the more suitable the fabric is for heavier usage.

Decorative
Less than 10,000 rubs

Light Domestic (occasional use upholstery)
10,000–15,000 rubs

General Domestic (everyday use upholstery)
15,000–25,000 rubs

Heavy Duty (high levels of everyday use)
25,000–30,000 rubs

Commercial Grade
30,000 plus rubs

Railroading

If you are upholstering a larger item, such as a sofa, it's a good idea to see if the fabric you are buying can be railroaded. Railroading refers to being able to turn the fabric to run from left to right, rather than the conventional top to bottom. For a fabric with a standard working width of 137cm (54in) (taking into account the seam or turning allowance of 3cm/1⅛in), you would have to create a seam to join the fabric to fit the width of the sofa, but when a pattern is railroaded you can turn it on its side and roll it out to the width of the sofa without join lines.

   This really only applies to heavily patterned fabrics. If you are using a woven or plain fabric, you normally won't have to worry. Having said that, just by rolling the fabric out from the roll, you will be able to see if the pile looks drastically different railroaded.

Fabric was railroaded on the mid-century sofa.

Treated Fabric for Fire Retardancy

To make furniture fire retardant you can buy fabric which has been specially treated: for heavy contract upholstery fabrics, this usually has a rubber-like coating attached to the back of the fabric. If it is not rated, you can have your chosen fabric made fire retardant by paying extra to get it chemically treated, although this is not suitable for fine fabrics and some velvets.

   For the featured projects, I have used a fire-retardant calico as the barrier cloth, and by applying a top fabric with a natural fibre content of over 75 per cent (which has been cigarette tested) this means the furniture complies with fire regulations in the United Kingdom (for domestic use). However, it is important to check the fire-regulation compliancy in your country as these can differ considerably.

Limited Purchase Quantity

If you are buying online, most fabric companies will have a limited purchase quantity of 1m (1yd), so if you only require a small piece, for the lid of a laundry bin for example, it may be best to buy from a store. The standard width for new upholstery fabric is 140cm (55in).

Cutting and Carriage Costs

When purchasing upholstery online, you may incur cutting and carriage charges. Make sure you are aware of any extra costs up front; the supplier may have a flat rate whether you buy just one metre or yard, or 15, and this can add quite a bit to the overall cost of a project.

Buying Vintage Fabric

I source vintage fabric in the same way I look for furniture – at flea markets, second-hand stores and auction sites. More recently I have discovered that, if I want to buy good quality vintage fabrics, I need to buy online where a detailed description is given, or at specialist vintage stores. Even so, you will have to be the final judge of a fabric's suitability, so here is what to look out for.

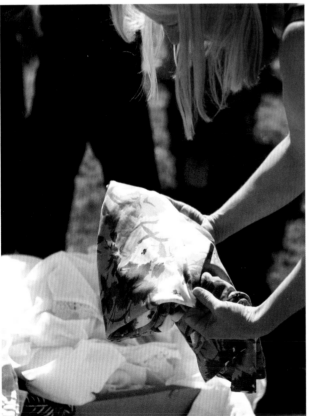

If you can find an upholstery weight vintage fabric large enough to cover a chair, it will most likely cost you a lot less than buying new, and will certainly make your piece unique.

Is It Upholstery Fabric?

Ideally you want a thicker fabric, so pop it between your finger and thumb and rub together. Curtains are often a good starting point as they tend to be a heavier weight and you get quite a lot of fabric in a curtain length. But the best type of fabric to buy for upholstery is an unused one that has been kept on its bolt. Most of the vintage fabric I buy from the 1960s and 1970s has its composition written on the selvedge, so I know what its content is.

Width and Length

Vintage fabrics from the 1960s or 1970s tend to have narrower widths of between 113–122cm (45–48in), and this will affect how much of a chair you can upholster with your vintage fabric.

If you are looking for lengths of more than 2m (2⅛yd), try going online to a specialist vintage fabric shop that sells unused bolts of vintage fabrics.

Wear and Tear

Check fabric carefully before purchasing it. Hold it up to the light to check that it is not too worn. Holes can result from the break up of the fibres over time, or from insects such as moths, which is something to be particularly vigilant of if you are buying vintage heavy wool fabrics. Keep a look out for stains – if you see tiny dark tan stains, these are likely to be rust spots that are virtually impossible to remove.

Laundering

Vintage fabrics often smell musty. If the fabric is previously unused, often just pegging it out on the washing line and spraying it with scented water can freshen it up. To get rid of more persistent smells, I hand wash used fabrics and dry them on the line, or I soak them in borax, which is a gentle, effective detergent.

TOOLS AND MATERIALS

In this section I introduce you to the tools and materials I use everyday. My basic toolkit has everything required, from stripping down tools to putting-back-together-again tools and the basic stuffing and materials that I use to build up the layers on the furniture in this book. The basic sewing kit covers what you might need when applying the finishing touches to a chair, and there is also some information about decorative trims.

BASIC TOOLKIT

A tool is a personal object: what suits the hand of one person can be weighty in the hand of another. I have small hands and prefer my tools to be lightweight, so I find smaller mallets and hand tools work for me. I also prefer wooden handles, but you may choose to go with an angled plastic handle which can provide a better grip. If you can, try out the options to find what works best for you before buying.

I have divided the tools into four categories for the stages when you are most likely to use them when making the projects in this book – tools for stripping down, repair, re-assembly and finishing touches – however, some tools, such as scissors and needles, are interchangeable.

Tools for Stripping Down

Mallet Use a wooden mallet, in conjunction with a staple remover or tack remover and pliers, to remove layers when stripping the chair back to the frame. The mallet pictured is a smaller style, but they are available in varying sizes.

Tack remover and staple remover The V-shaped blade on the tack remover allows you to flick up tacks, whilst the flat-headed staple remover allows you to lever under staples.

Pliers These pointed pliers are ideal for removing staples during the stripping process, although regular pliers, and also pincers, do the job.

Screwdriver Use to take off lids and legs when stripping down furniture: both flat head and Philips are required.

Tools for Repair

Sandpaper For rubbing down furniture after it has been stripped; I use fine grain mostly, but keep a selection of different grades available.

Paintbrush For touching up varnish on the legs and arms of furniture.

Tools for Re-assembly

Magnetic tack hammer This is particularly useful for putting in tacks or gimp pins: the magnetic end of the head allows you to hold the tack steady and tap it into the frame; then the head is turned to hammer the tack in fully. When using to fix decorative tacks, wrap the hammer head with calico or wadding and knock in gently. This tool can also be used to hit in stubborn staples that don't quite go all the way into the frame.

Regulator Generally used to shift stuffing around under a seat; I also use the flat end of the tool to tuck under the fold when buttoning and to help with pleated corners.

Metrer ruler (yardstick) and tape measure Both are consistently used throughout the upholstering process. I have a tape measure permanently draped around my neck, and you'll find a metal or wooden metre ruler (yardstick) becomes your best friend when measuring fabric for cutting.

Web stretcher Use to stretch the webbing tightly across a frame.

Button needle A very long needle used to draw button twine all the way through the upholstery layers when attaching a button. Straight button needles are available but a bayonet (square point) button needle is shown in the photograph, and its sharp square end is particularly good for thick, deep layers.

Scissors A pair of large heavy duty scissors will cut through leather and thin foam, and you can also use them to cut top fabric. A good pair will be expensive, but keep them sharpened and they will go on and on.

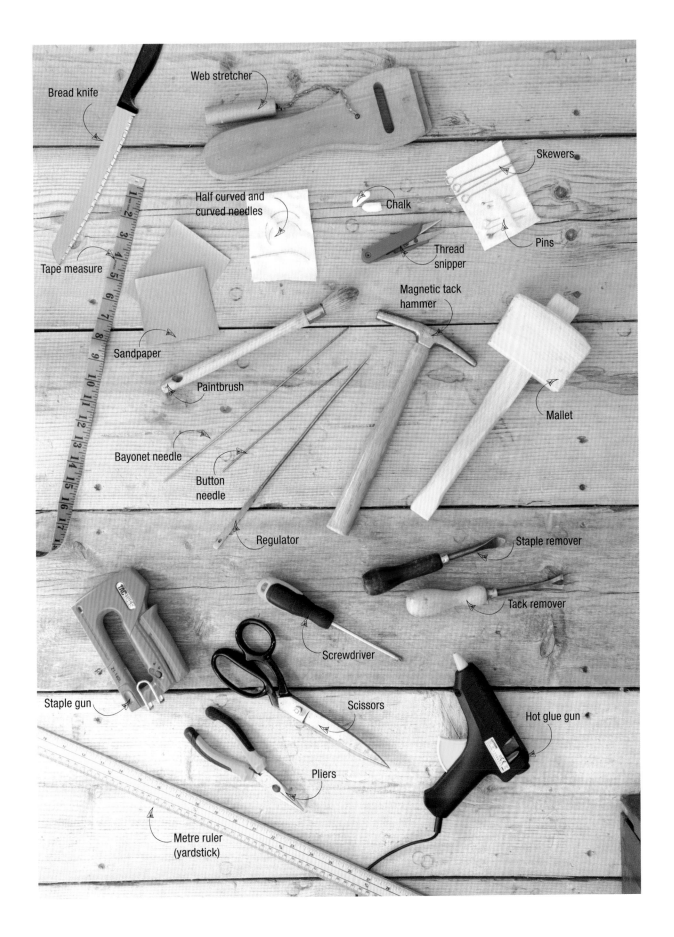

Bread knife

Web stretcher

Skewers

Half curved and curved needles

Chalk

Pins

Tape measure

Thread snipper

Magnetic tack hammer

Sandpaper

Paintbrush

Mallet

Bayonet needle

Button needle

Regulator

Staple remover

Tack remover

Screwdriver

Staple gun

Scissors

Hot glue gun

Pliers

Metre ruler (yardstick)

Chalk I use chalk to mark fabric as it is easy to rub off, but there are other options you may prefer including water-erasable marker pens or tailor's chalk.

Staple gun An example of a basic hand-held staple gun suitable for upholstery is shown in the photograph: choose one that can take staple sizes ranging from 6–10mm (¼–⅜in). An electric staple gun is a little more expensive, but it is definitely worth the investment if you are taking on more or larger upholstery projects – it provides more power so there is less strain on your arms. I used a pneumatic staple gun for upholstering the featured projects, but they can all be achieved using either a hand-held or an electric staple gun.

Bread knife Use to cut foam; an electric bread knife is useful for larger projects.

Thread snippers Use to make release cuts and to trim stray threads.

Tools for the Finishing Touches

Hot glue gun A quick and easy fix for adding double piping and braiding to add the finishing touches to your chair. Be careful not to drip the glue on your skin – it gets VERY hot!

Half-curved and curved needles Half-curved needles are particularly useful at the building up stage of upholstery when springs are involved, while curved needles are used to sew slip stitches when finishing off a chair. It's best to have a variety of sizes: use the smaller needles to get a neater look for the finishing touches.

Pins and skewers You'll need pins to hold your fabric when machine sewing, and medium or large skewers to hold fabric layers in place when hand stitching directly onto the furniture.

Tip

It is much healthier to work in a well-ventilated space so keep a window or door open.

Basic Health and Safety Kit

Apron Taking apart a chair can be a mucky business, and wearing an apron will give your clothes and you some added protection from splinters and hot glue drips.

Safety glasses These will protect your eyes when you are flicking staples out of a frame during the stripping down process.

Dust mask I often wear a dust mask when I'm stripping down older chairs as you can never be quite sure what you are dealing with.

Gloves Use leather or golf gloves for stripping down furniture to avoid blisters. Plastic gloves are useful to protect your hands when using spray glue, paint stripper or varnish.

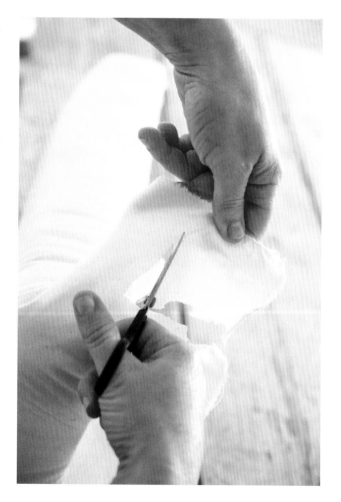

BASIC SEWING KIT

Some of the needles and threads in this basic sewing kit have been mentioned before, but here the focus is on using them for finishing techniques.

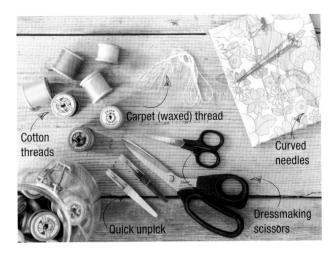

Curved needles Small curved needles are better for slip stitch and the larger ones are useful if you have a lot of layers, or if you are using a thick top fabric, such as a woven wool fabric.

Cotton threads I love the colourful cotton reels often found in second-hand shops. I might use the thread for sewing projects such as decorative cushions, and if an edge is delicate and a fabric is thin, I may even use it instead of carpet (waxed) thread to sew up furniture. However, when I am sewing up a box cushion, I use a thicker upholstery thread as it doesn't snap as easily.

Carpet (waxed) thread This heavy-duty thread, available in different colours, is ideal for hand stitching thick upholstery fabrics.

Dressmaking scissors A heavyweight pair is good for cutting fabric lengths, but a medium-weight pair with sharp tips is best for cutting fabric when it has been applied to the chair. Smaller pairs are useful for thread snipping, and I use pinking shears (not shown) to reduce fraying on the seams of sewn fabric.

Sewing machine This is key for making piping, putting in a zip, or making cushions. Apart from a straight sewing foot, a zip foot and/or a piping foot are useful.

Quick unpick A useful little tool that provides extra help in the stripping down phase, or for unpicking when things don't go right the first time on the sewing machine!

Equipment Around the House

There are a few other things you might need that in all likelihood you will have around the home already:

Apron As well as a stripping down furniture apron, keep a separate re-assembly apron to hand. Often when sewing up a box cushion or cutting a fabric you will get littered with threads.

Iron and ironing board I drag my ironing board out to my studio fairly regularly. Most of the time the action of pulling the fabric taut over your furniture will dissolve any creases, but you will always get those fabrics that need an extra iron before application.

Notepad and pencil I like to make notes when stripping a chair as well as taking down measurements during the upholstery process. It's worth keeping a notepad handy when you are upholstering.

Drill Occasionally you need to use a drill, perhaps to make a hole in the base of the furniture to add buttons. Use a drill with a wood drill bit. I also use my drill for screwing in legs, it's a real time saver.

Cleaning and oiling products An excellent mix for cleaning grime off furniture legs is a homemade mixture I refer to as 'magi mix'. It is one part white spirit (mineral spirits), one part raw linseed oil, one part white vinegar and one part methylated spirits (de-natured alcohol). Mix it in a glass container and rub it on with either a rag or wire wool, but be sure to wear protective rubber gloves.

My trusty 1980s Semi-Industrial New Home sewing machine has served me well over the years. I use straight stitch and zigzag for overlocking edges.

BASIC STUFFING AND MATERIALS

Below I have outlined everything I use to stuff and build up the layers on the projects featured in this book. These fillings and materials are appropriate for the modern upholstery methods I have used, but they are by no means exhaustive. As you take apart your chair, don't be surprised to find all sorts of unusual stuffing, from straw to coconut coir. In the upholstery in this book, I only use foam, as it's easy to access and quick and appropriate for the furniture I have selected. For more information about some of these materials see Techniques: Layers in Upholstery.

Webbing There are lots of different types available in a variety of widths, but for the featured projects I have used only 5cm (2in) wide jute webbing. Other styles you might come across include black-and-white herringbone, used for extra strength, and rubber Pirelli, an elasticated rubber webbing often seen on the base of an Ercol sofa.

Hessian (burlap) Available in different thicknesses, this is used to cover webbing or springs and as a base layer for all other stuffing. I used 340g (12oz) for the featured projects, which has a tighter weave, but 283g (10oz) hessian would also be appropriate.

Foam This is available in different thicknesses and weights depending on its application, and it can be cut to virtually any size and shape. For the featured projects I mainly used blue or grey foam – blue foam is one of the hardest foams you can buy – and for seat box cushions I use a softer gold foam.

Stockinette A single jersey knit fabric used to hold foam cushion interiors in place; buy it from the roll in metre (yard) lengths.

Polyester wadding Sometimes referred to as Dacron, this is used over foam and calico to pad and provide extra comfort. Wadding comes in different thicknesses and widths, including longer widths. For the featured projects, I have used layered 56g (2oz) polyester wadding on a short 67cm (26in) width.

Calico An inexpensive unbleached cotton fabric that is used as a lining material in upholstery. I use fire-retardant calico in all my projects as a barrier cloth before applying top fabric. Calico is sold in double or single widths of 150cm (59in).

Platform cloth You may also hear this referred to as the bottoming cloth or dust cover, and for modern upholstery, either black cotton or Dipryl is generally used. Dipryl is a synthetic bonded material which is both cheap and effective, but I prefer to use a black cotton (also available in beige and brown). Platform cloth comes in a standard 140cm (55in) width and can be bought by the metre (yard).

Tacks Tacks come in various sizes and for the featured projects I have used large 16i tacks to attach laid cord. Tacks can be used instead of staples to attach layers and fabrics.

Staples I use three sizes of staple for the featured projects: 6mm (¼in), 8mm (⁵⁄₁₆in) and 10mm (³⁄₈in). The longer the length of the shaft, the more layers it can hold. The staple lengths I give are intended as a guide but you should use your own judgment depending on the materials you are using. An average box contains 10,000 staples in pre-formed magazine lengths.

Varnish Use to freshen up the wood on the legs and arms of a chair. Tinted or clear varnish, linseed oil or wax can be used depending on your preferred look.

PVA glue and sawdust When mixed together, PVA glue and fine sawdust makes an excellent wood filler for filling deep tack holes in your stripped furniture frame (see Techniques: Stripping and Filling).

Button twine This is a thick white nylon twine used to attach buttons to furniture. It can be bought by the metre (yard) and comes on 250g (8½oz) cops.

Upholstery twine This is available in different strengths: I have used the strongest, cord twine no. 4, which is good for sewing in springs. It is generally bought in 250g (8½oz) balls.

Carpet thread (waxed thread) A heavy hand-sewing thread used to stitch two pieces of fabric together, usually with slip stitch. Available in light or dark colour tones, buy it in 500g (17oz) cops or in a bunch of single threads

Laid (lacing) cord This is used to secure springs to a chair frame; it is sold in large 600g (21oz) balls.

Spray glue This can be bought in different strengths – I use carpet adhesive or car trim spray glue. Always use it outdoors and once the spray glue is applied, leave

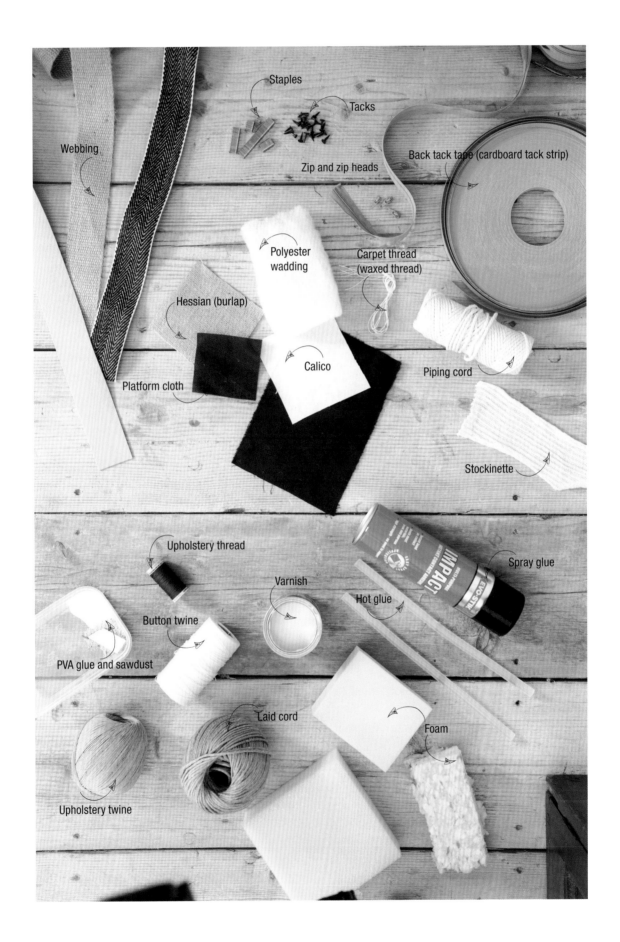

Staples

Tacks

Webbing

Zip and zip heads

Back tack tape (cardboard tack strip)

Polyester wadding

Carpet thread (waxed thread)

Hessian (burlap)

Calico

Piping cord

Platform cloth

Stockinette

Upholstery thread

Spray glue

Varnish

Hot glue

Button twine

PVA glue and sawdust

Laid cord

Foam

Upholstery twine

the sprayed material for 30 seconds before the final application to make sure it is really tacky.

Hot glue This can be purchased in packs of 10 in short or long lengths, to be used with a hot glue gun.

Piping cord (welt cord) I have used an unbleached, medium-weight, cotton-twist piping cord that is pre-shrunk, bought in 1kg (2.2lb) cops; fine and heavy piping cord weights are also available.

Back tacktape (cardboard tack strip) This thick cardboard strip allows you to staple fabric to an edge without the need for hand sewing. It measures 1.25cm (½in) wide and is bought on 10m (11yd) rolls.

Zip and zip heads Continuous zipping is useful in upholstery work as you can cut it to the length you require. It's used with smaller and larger zip heads and comes in a range of dark and light tones. It can be bought in shorter 1m (1yd) lengths.

Upholstery Thread I use a range of threads, depending on the project: 100 per cent polyester upholstery thread is perfect for my semi-industrial sewing machine; I also use nylon-bonded thread. Thread colour can be matched exactly to your top fabric.

TRIMS AND TACKS

If you have unwanted staples on show on a noticeable part of your chair, such as around the legs, arms or seat rim, or if you are just looking to add detail to your furniture, you can add a decorative trim or tacks.

Decorative Tacks

There are many choices of colour and size and decorative tacks can easily be purchased online or in your local haberdashery or hardware store. They can be bought in packs of 25 upwards and applied individually directly next to each other or evenly spaced. For quick and easy application, strips of attached tacks (nail strip) are also available. Both types are applied with a magnetic tack hammer (see Basic Toolkit).

Metallic tacks For a more traditional look antique bronze, copper or gold finish tacks are a good choice.

Colour coated tacks Choose your tacks to match your top fabric for a more contemporary look and feel.

Nail strip Available as a minimum 1m (1yd) length, this decorative strip is used in modern upholstery for a speedy, consistent application of tacks. The strips consist of faux tacks, and in every fifth link of the strip there is a link with a hole into which a matching tack is added to fix the strip in place.

Tip

Its surprising how many tacks you will need to go around an edge, so do make sure you measure the area to work out how many you will need.

Trims

Furniture trims go in and out of fashion, but generally you can find fringes, braids and cord. Trimmings can be attached with either a hot glue gun or with gimp pins, or both. Keep the trim on the roll as you add it to the furniture to avoid cutting it too short as it does stretch a little as you apply it. The hot glue dries very quickly so apply a little at a time, adding braid in sections of 3–5cm (1⅛–2in) at a time.

Fringe This can be applied to elongate the fabric, usually at the base of the furniture to cover wheels. You can buy some fantastic designs.

Braiding This is available in different thicknesses and all sorts of delightful colours. It comes plaited and has feature edges in some cases.

Gimp pins These are small sharp tacks applied with a magnetic tack hammer to attach braiding in place or to make glued-on braiding extra secure. The small head and colour tone make them almost invisible, and you can also use them on a show edge to attach the fabric where there is no other alternative. Apply about 2.5cm (1in) apart, or wider if tacking in over glued-on braiding.

Buttons

There are several ways to make buttons for upholstery and I show you how to make some simple large buttons in the Techniques section of this book. Other options are also covered there (see Techniques: Buttons).

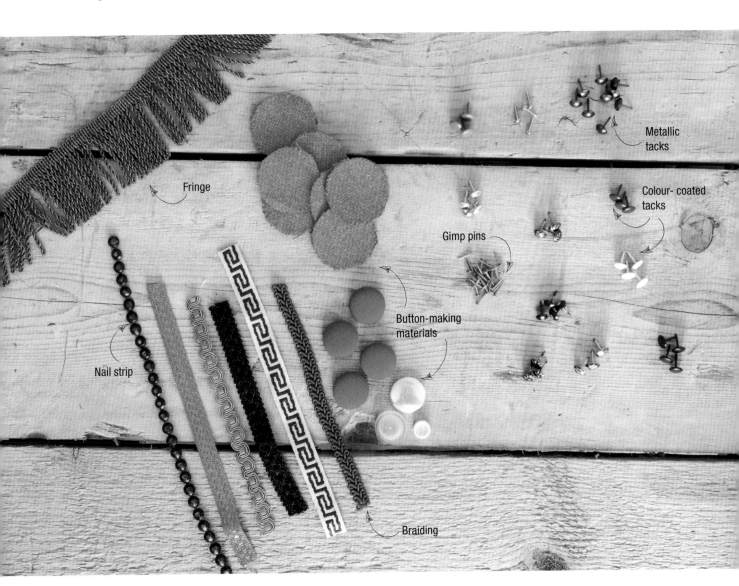

Fringe

Metallic tacks

Colour- coated tacks

Gimp pins

Button-making materials

Nail strip

Braiding

PROJECTS

In this Projects section I take you through the processes of stripping down and re-assembling ten furniture projects step by step, starting with smaller pieces to ease you in, and gradually working up to slightly more challenging projects.

Chosen Just for You

I do like my furniture to be practical, and I am always looking for storage solutions around my home, and with this in mind, I've chosen a few pieces that are both practical and pretty. These include reupholstering the lid of an old laundry bin for a practical storage unit for your bathroom that doubles as a seat – perfect for when you are bathing the kids – and a blanket box to store your surplus linens. I've included projects for every room of the house, including a sofa for your lounge, a nursery chair for the playroom and a headboard for your bedroom.

Supporting You Through the Process

All the furniture in this book is upholstered with foam stuffing and attached with staples, and I use the same basic toolkit for each project, so there are no surprises. My aim has been to keep it simple and to guide you by example. So, to support the illustrated step-by-step project instructions, I've filmed myself upholstering and sewing each of the featured projects with a time-lapse video. I've also identified key techniques (see Techniques) and referenced these in the project text, and each is illustrated with detailed close-up photos to explain the upholstery processes used.

I've provided the quantities I have used for the stuffing and materials for each project, but these should be used as a guide only. Once you have your piece of furniture home, armed with a tape measure, you can determine exactly the quantities you will need. As you progress through the projects, you will be building on your upholstering skills, and this will give you the confidence to apply the processes to your own furniture projects.

Fabric choice is, of course, subjective, so for each project I've included a Fabric Focus feature to help you visualize other fabrics that would suit the style of furniture. (For details, see Suppliers).

LAUNDRY BIN

A vintage wicker laundry bin is perfect for bathroom storage, particularly if you have small children and a lot of bath toys! Simply spray paint the base, make a domed lid and attach some vintage towelling fabric for a quick transformation that is both practical and comfortable. Laundry bins from the 1940s come in lots of different shapes and sizes, and some may have legs, so look for one to suit your space and style. You may find one that has a hard wooden base, and this will look lovely painted or upholstered.

Vintage hinge-lid laundry bins are ideal for storage and will also double up as seats. With its original 1940s paint finish and the lid fabric ripped off, this one was uncomfortable, tatty and in need of a makeover.

THE WICKER HAS BEEN GIVEN A FRESH LICK OF PAINT AND THE BRIGHTLY UPHOLSTERED TOWELLING LID IS BOTH PRACTICAL AND COMFY.

Watch my time-lapse video of this project from start to finish. Scan this QR code or key the following into your browser. http://youtu.be/qV8SSkFmvyo

Fabric Focus

TOOLS AND MATERIALS

Basic toolkit

Basic health and safety kit

Upholstery weight fabric, 50cmL x 120cmW (20inL x 47inW)

Fire-retardant calico, 50cmL x 75cmW (20inL x 29inW)

56g (2oz) polyester wadding (batting), 100cmL x 67cmW (39inL x 26inW)

2.5cm (1in) grey foam, one sheet measuring 100cm (39in) square

Size 6mm (¼in) and 8mm (⁵⁄₁₆in) staples, one box each

Back tack tape (cardboard tack strip), 50cm (20in)

Carpet thread (waxed thread), 100cm (39in)

Canvas ribbon, 25cm (9in)

Spray glue

Notepad and pencil

Wood filler (optional

Wood glue (optional)

Spray paint for base (optional)

Measuring Up

You will only need about 0.5m (20in) of fabric for this laundry lid, and you could choose a different fabric for the inside of the lid. Take the measurements across the top and the inside of the lid. (For extra help see Techniques: Measuring and Cutting Fabric.)

Stripping Down

Unscrew the lid from the base and, leaving the hinges in place, remove any remaining fabric: use a tack or staple remover and mallet, and pull out any stubborn tacks or staples with pliers (see Techniques: Stripping and Filling). Dispose of all materials.

Tip

It's all too easy to sweep up the screws with the rest of the debris from the lid, so make sure to put them in a safe place.

Repairs

These wicker laundry bins usually sit on small wooden feet. Make sure these are still attached and if not, glue them in place to make them extra secure. If re-painting, the wicker is best sprayed to avoid paint build up in the gaps.

RE-ASSEMBLY

Domed lid

1 Chalk a rectangular shape roughly half the size of the lid in the centre of the top of the lid. Use the rectangular shape as a template to cut a piece of 2.5cm (1in) foam. Now use the lid itself as a template to cut out a second piece of 2.5cm (1in) foam (**A**).

2 In a well-ventilated area spray glue both pieces of foam on one side only, leave for 30 seconds to go tacky, then stick the smaller piece in the centre of the lid top and the larger piece on top of that (**B**). Trim off any foam that hangs over the edge with a bread knife or scissors.

3 Lay two layers of polyester wadding to fit over the top and sides of the lid. Pinch the wadding together at the corners and trim off any excess to reduce bulk.

4 Measure the lid across the top and over the edge to the inside of the lid and cut out the calico to size. Place the calico on your table and place the lid on top, covered side facing down. Starting at the middle of each edge, staple the calico in place using 6mm (¼in) staples. Pull the calico taut but not so tight that the calico buckles. Finish stapling along the curved edge, but leave the corners until last. On the back edge, cut around the hinges using a 'V' cut and fold the fabric at the corners using a bed sheet pleat (see Techniques: Fabric Cuts and Pleats) (**C**).

A

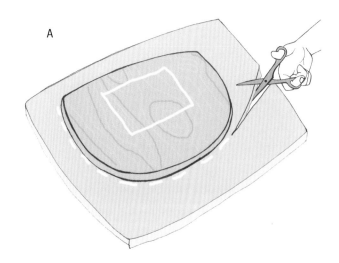

B

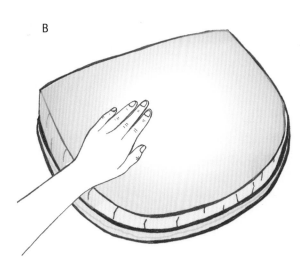

C

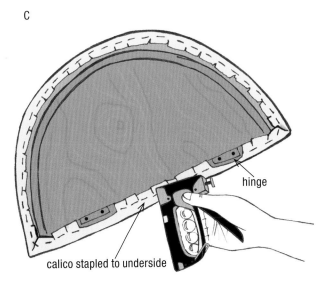

hinge

calico stapled to underside

Tip

If the calico starts to buckle the foam, remove the staples and re-apply to achieve a smooth dome shape.

5 Turn the lid topside up and add one layer of polyester wadding over the calico, cutting away any excess wadding that falls to the underside of the lid.

Adding Fabric

6 Measure across the top and down the sides of the lid, add turning allowance (about 3cm/1⅛in), then cut your fabric to the measured size.

Tip

To centre a patterned fabric before cutting it to size, place it over the lid and pin around the lid shape to mark your cutting line.

7 Staple the top fabric to the underside of the lid using 8mm (⁵⁄₁₆in) staples, start in the middle of each edge leaving the corners until last. Make 'V' cuts at the hinges (**D**) and fold the corners with a bed sheet pleat.

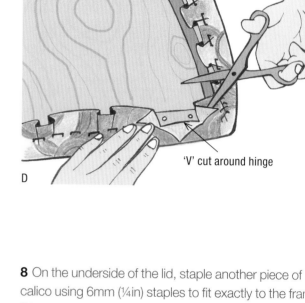

fabric stapled to underside

'V' cut around hinge

D

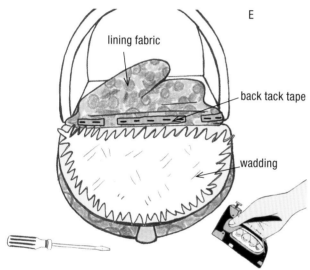

E

lining fabric

back tack tape

wadding

8 On the underside of the lid, staple another piece of calico using 6mm (¼in) staples to fit exactly to the frame. Trim off any excess. To make the tab to lift the lid, fold a piece of canvas ribbon in half, measure the mid point of the curved edge of the lid and staple the ribbon in place using 8mm (⁵⁄₁₆in) staples.

9 Measure the underside of the lid and cut another piece of fabric to line it. Before attaching the fabric, re-attach the lid to the base of the laundry bin. Use back tack tape and 8mm (⁵⁄₁₆in) staples to attach the fabric to line the lid (see Techniques: Back Tack Tape): make sure the back tack tape doesn't get placed over the hinges by leaving spaces as you staple it in (**E**). Add one layer of polyester wadding to fit the underside of the lid.

Tip

Make sure you pull the hinges out from the underside of the lid before you add the back tack tape.

LAUNDRY BIN

10 Pull the lining fabric over and carefully pin it to the underside of the lid tucking the edges under as you go; use medium-sized pins placed about 3cm (1⅛in) apart (**F**). To ensure the lining fabric fits smoothly to the curved edge of the frame, it may be necessary to make some release cuts in the turning allowance.

F

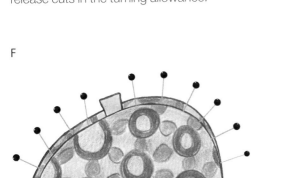

The Finishing Touches

11 Using a small curved needle and some carpet thread, sew the lining in place with slip stitch all the way around the edge, pulling out the pins as you go (see Techniques: Knots and Stitches).

DANISH-STYLE DINING CHAIR

Dining chairs from the 1960s were slim and slender with elegant tapered legs, as furniture manufacturers looked to Danish design for inspiration. This mid-century British-made McIntosh dining chair would have been part of a set of six, but its unique style and comfortable backrest make it perfect for a stand alone office chair. The wood frame – a beautiful rosewood – just requires a little oiling, and other frames may be found in lighter wood such as elm. I've used a bright yellow geometric pattern for the reupholstery.

The beautiful bone structure of this dining chair is lost in its little black dress.

THE VIBRANT FABRIC MAKES THIS CHAIR, ONCE PART OF A SET OF SIX, STAND OUT ON ITS OWN.

Watch my time-lapse video of this project from start to finish. Scan this QR code or key the following into your browser. http://youtu.be/UiV1cw4Si0U

Fabric Focus

TOOLS AND MATERIALS

Basic toolkit

Basic health and safety kit

Upholstery weight fabric, 75cmL x 140cmW (29inL x 55inW)

Fire-retardant calico, 50cmL x 75cmW (20inL x 29inW)

Platform cloth, 50cm (20in) square

56g (2oz) polyester waddin (batting), 150cmL x 67cmW (59inL x 26inW)

2.5cm (1in) grey foam, one sheet measuring 60cm (23in) square

1.25cm (½in) blue foam, one sheet measuring 50cm (20in) square

Size 6mm (¼in) and 8mm (⁵⁄₁₆in) staples, one box each

Medium piping cord, 100cm (39in)

Carpet thread (waxed thread), 100cm (39in)

Gimp pins, 10

Spray glue

Notepad and pencil

Woodfiller (optional)

Linseed oil (optional)

Measuring Up

This dining chair is unlikely to require more than a metre of fabric. To establish exactly how much fabric you will need, first measure the seat width and length, adding a turning allowance of about 3cm (1⅛in) to fix the fabric to the underside of the seat. For the backrest you will use one continuous piece of fabric: measure the length and width taking the tape measure from front to back and add a small turning allowance of 1.5cm (⅝in) to each edge. The side edges of the backrest will be covered with double piping, so measure the length and calculate your fabric requirements for covering the piping cord. (See Techniques: Measuring and Cutting Fabric and Techniques: Single and Double Piping for more guidance.)

Stripping Down

Some chairs from this era have a seat that drops into the frame surround, but the seat on this chair is screwed in. Unscrew the seat and start to take off the fabric from the underside: use a staple remover and mallet, and pull out any stubborn tacks or staples with pliers (see Techniques: Stripping and Filling).

Dispose of all materials from the stripped seat, then move on to the backrest. This is stapled to the frame underneath the backrest so turn the chair over. Start by removing the piping strip around the edges, then work across from left to right removing all the staples.

Repairs

Designed and made in the 1960s, this McIntosh dining chair is made from rosewood and oiled rather than stained. If there is a lot of damage to the legs of the chair, it could be lightly sanded and stained, but this one only required a light oiling using linseed oil as the rosewood colour is such a beautiful tone. The top fabric is likely to have been stapled, so there should be little structural damage to the chair frame.

Tip

Use a scrap piece of calico to rub down the frame with linseed oil.

RE-ASSEMBLY

Seat Base

1 Place the seat base on top of the 2.5cm (1in) foam, draw around it and cut it out. Working in a well-ventilated area, spray glue one side of the foam, leave for 30 seconds until it is really tacky, then stick it to the top of the seat base (**A**).

2 Apply two pieces of polyester wadding to fit over the foam, pinching the corners to remove any excess wadding and cutting or tearing any excess from the underside of the seat.

3 Measure the seat again over the top of the foam to the underside, and cut some calico to fit adding a 3cm (1⅛in) turning allowance all around. Lay the calico on your table and place the seat base in the middle so the underside is facing you. Using size 6mm (¼in) staples, begin to staple the calico in place approximately 1.5cm (⅝in) from the edge, starting from the middle of each side and pulling the calico taut, but not so tight that the foam bulges and ripples. Staple first along one side, then along the opposite side until you get close to | each corner (**B**). The corners are not pleated: just grab the calico in your hand and pull tight on the corner – the calico will ruffle on the underside, but this should not show on the topside – and staple each corner down. Trim any excess calico and make sure the screw holes are uncovered.

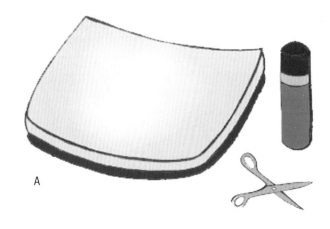

A

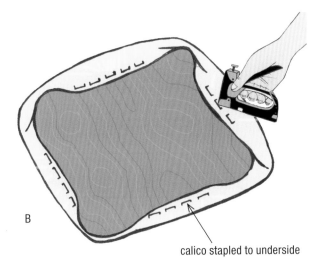

B

calico stapled to underside

Backrest

4 Now move on to the backrest. Measure the length of the backrest from front to back and then the width. Draw this shape onto 1.25cm (½in) foam and cut out. Spray glue the foam on one side and leave for 30 seconds to go tacky. Stick it to the front of the backrest and fold it over to the back. Staple it in place along the side and bottom edges using 8mm (⁵⁄₁₆in) staples (**C**).

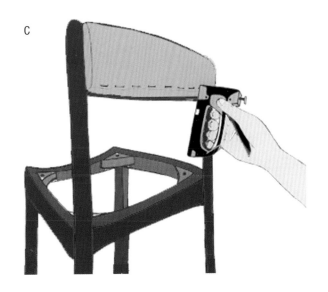

C

5 Add two layers of polyester wadding to cover the foam, tearing off any excess around the frame.

6 Measure the backrest again over the top of the foam from front to back and cut some calico to fit the exact shape. Staple this along the sides and the bottom front and back edges using size 8mm (⁵⁄₁₆in) staples (**D**).

Adding Fabric

7 Starting on the seat base, measure across the seat around to the underside, allowing an extra 3cm (1⅛in) for turning allowances all the way around, and cut your fabric out.

8 Add one layer of polyester wadding over the top of the calico, trimming away any excess wadding that falls to the underside of the seat.

9 Lay your fabric face down on the table and place the seat base in the middle so the underside is facing you. Staple the fabric in place as you did the calico using 6mm (¼in) staples (see step 3), work from the middle of each edge, first on one side, then the opposite side, to the corners (**E**). At the corners grab the fabric and pull taut making sure the pleats form on the underside of the seat only (check that the topside is smooth) and staple the corners in place. Trim excess fabric.

D

10 Moving on to the backrest, measure the backrest and allowing for a turning allowance of 3cm (1⅛in) to the length, cut your fabric.

11 Add one layer of polyester wadding to cover over the calico, trimming off excess where necessary.

12 Take your fabric and start by stapling it onto the underside of the back edge working from the middle out using 8mm (⁵⁄₁₆in) staples and stopping about 5cm (2in) from the sides. On the front edge, fold the fabric under and place over the stapled back edge. Begin stapling from the middle, stopping 5cm (2in) from the sides, as before – see (**F**) for finished look.

13 At the side, fold the fabric under and staple very close to the edge making sure not to distort the fabric. Once each side edge of the backrest has been stapled, finish stapling the underside (**F**).

fabric pleats on underside only

E

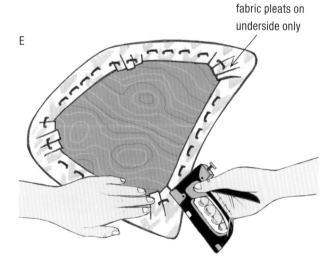

F

fabric folded and attached at base

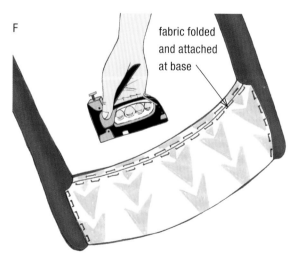

16 To fix the piping to the backrest, find the mid point of the piping length. With the mid point positioned at the top edge of the backrest, start gluing it down the front no more than 2.5cm (1in) at a time, then down the back. Trim off any excess piping and secure the piping to the underside of the backrest with a couple of staples or gimp pins.

Tip

If you find you have lots of piping left, unpick the ends and remove some of the piping cord so it folds neatly under at the bottom edge.

The Finishing Touches

14 To finish off the backrest, add a strip of double piping around the sides. Plug in your hot glue gun to give it time to warm up while you make the piping.

15 Measure the length of the backrest from back to front and use this measurement to cut the fabric for each length of the piping. For instructions on how to make double piping see Techniques: Single and Double Piping.

17 Now to finish the seat. Turn the seat over to measure the base for cutting the platform cloth allowing for a 1.5cm (⅝in) turning allowance. Place the cut out platform cloth over the base and start by stapling it in the middle of each edge using size 8mm (⁵⁄₁₆in) staples. Work your way along the edge pulling the platform cloth taut so no ruffles appear. Find the screw holes with your fingers and make little cross-shaped release cuts with a quick unpick so you can get the screws in without catching the fabric. Screw the seat back into the frame.

BLANKET BOX

Plastic-coated ottomans from the 1950s are the perfect shape and size for storing toys, linen or craft supplies. Two complementary fabrics can be added to the base and lid to match your room's colour scheme, and as the upholstery process is relatively simple, the transformation can be achieved fairly quickly. I have created a domed lid for extra comfort using a geometric print for the outside of the lid and a gorgeous pastel pink print for the base and lid lining.

The 1950s style and the tapered legs make this blanket box appeal aesthetically, but with its plastic coat it is shouting out to be made into something a little less clinical.

THE BLANKET BOX HAS BEEN TRANSFORMED INTO A USEFUL STORAGE UNIT AND A COMFY SEAT

Watch my time-lapse video of this project from start to finish. Scan this QR code or key the following into your browser: http://youtu.be/-VdyrUdU0mo

Fabric Focus

So many choices: a vintage novelty print for a playroom, an opulent velvet for the bedroom, or a retro barkcloth, perfect for the fabric hoarder.

TOOLS AND MATERIALS

Basic toolkit

Basic health and safety kit

Upholstery weight fabric, 150cmL x 140cmW (59inL x 55inW) or 225cm x 140cmW (88inL x 55inW) railroaded

Fire-retardant calico, 150cm (59in) square

Platform cloth, 1mL x 50cm (39inL x 20inW)

56g (2oz) polyester wadding, 8mL x 67cmW (8¾ydL x 26inW)

2.5cm (1in) grey foam, pre-cut to 100cmL x 50cmW (39inL x 20inW)

1.25cm (½in) blue foam, one sheet measuring 150cm (59in) square

Size 6mm (¼in) and 8mm (⁵⁄₁₆in) staples, one box each

Back tack tape (cardboard tack strip), 4m (4⅜yd)

Carpet thread (waxed thread), 100cm (39in)

Spray glue

Notepad and pencil

Wood filler (optional)

White spray paint

Measuring Up

Before you measure up, decide how you want to place your fabric onto the base of the box. This can be done in four separate sections, or the fabric can be railroaded (as I have done) to attach it in one length around the front and side edges, placing a separate section on the back. Measure the blanket box all the way around the base, and measure both the inside and the outside of the lid. Create a fabric cutting plan (see Techniques: Measuring and Cutting Fabric).

Adding foam to the base as I have done creates a thicker, puffier look, so make sure to allow for extra allowance on the fabric. Leave the cutting of the fabric until you have added the calico.

Stripping Down

Unscrew the lid and put the screws in a safe place. Using a tack or staple remover and mallet, remove the plastic coating from the base first, then use pliers to pull on the braiding around the top edge and try to rip it off in one piece. Remove the cover from the lid. Check that

all the staples have been removed from the base and lid, pulling out any that remain with pliers. Dispose of all fillings and covers. If the legs unscrew, remove them.

Repairs

My ottoman has removable tapered legs, but you can also find them with cabriole or square legs which are hidden. If the legs are attached you will need to undertake any repairs before upholstering, but if they can be removed, you can set them aside to work on later, re-spraying or re-varnishing as necessary. Whilst the frame is bare, spray the inside of the base with white spray paint, making sure to cover the top edges which will be seen when the lid is opened. Work outside and be sure to wear your mask – it's potent stuff.

Tip

Wear a mask when using spray paint and work outside.

RE-ASSEMBLY

Lid Section

1 Chalk a small rectangle in the centre of the top of the lid. Measure the rectangle and cut out the shape from the edge of your 2.5cm (1in) foam. Attach the foam in place with spray glue (**A**).

2 Place the remainder of the 2.5cm (1in) foam sheet on your table and place the lid on top of it, covered side facing down. Draw around the lid and cut out the shape. Spray glue the back of the foam, leave for 30 seconds to go tacky, then place it over the foam rectangle on top of the lid.

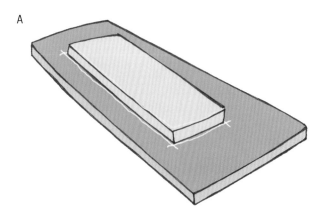
A

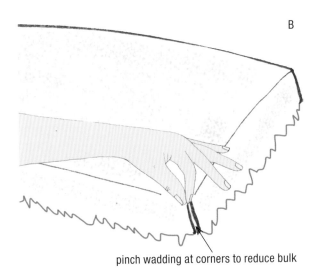
B

pinch wadding at corners to reduce bulk

3 Tear or cut two pieces of polyester wadding to fit the top and sides of the lid. Pull off any wadding from the underside of the lid and pinch the wadding over the corners to remove excess (**B**).

4 Measure and cut a piece of calico to fit over the top and sides, allowing for a turning allowance to attach it to the underside of the lid. Lay the calico on your table and place the lid on top, covered side facing down. Starting from the middle of each edge and working towards the corners, staple the calico in place using 6mm (¼in) staples. On the back edge, cut around the hinges using a 'V' cut, and at the corners, make a bed sheet pleat so the fold is visible from the side edge only (see Techniques: Fabric Cuts and Pleats) (**C**).

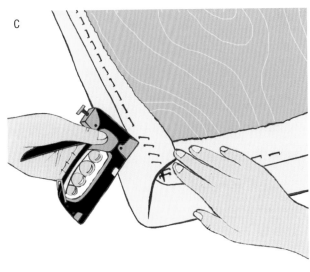
C

5 Turn the lid topside up and add one layer of polyester wadding over the calico, pinching the wadding over the corners to remove excess.

6 Measure across the lid to the underside and cut a piece of your fabric, with a turning allowance of 3cm (1.⅛in). Lay the fabric face down on the table and place the lid on top, covered side facing down. Starting from the middle of each edge, staple the fabric in place, as with the calico, making 'V' cuts around the hinges (**D**).

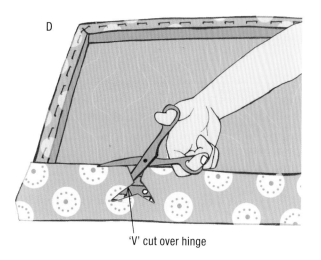

D

'V' cut over hinge

Tip

If you choose to, you can add single piping around the lid edge at this stage. Cut the piping into two pieces, one to fit between the hinges and one to go around the front edge and sides. (See Techniques: Single and Double Piping.)

7 Turn the lid over and cut a piece of calico to exactly fit the underside. Staple the calico in place using size 6mm (¼in) staples (**E**).

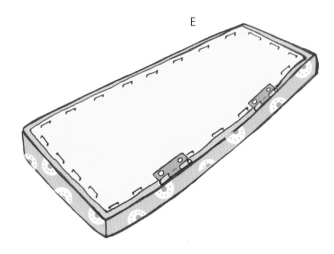

E

8 Measure and cut the fabric for the inside of the lid, allowing for at least a 1.5cm (⅝in) turning allowance. Along the back edge of the lid, apply back tack tape to the wrong side of the fabric in between and to either side of the hinges (see Techniques: Back Tack Tape).

9 Add a piece of polyester wadding over the calico and fold the attached fabric over it. Pin around the sides and front edge (**F**) turning the fabric edges under and pulling taut as you go. Set the lid aside.

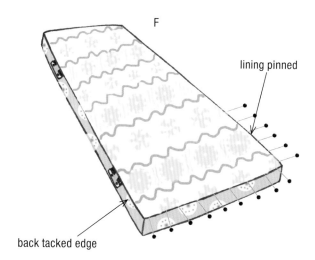

F

lining pinned

back tacked edge

Base Section

10 Measure the outside of the base and cut two pieces of 1.25cm (½in) foam to fit, one piece for the front and sides and one for the back. Working in a well-ventilated area, spray glue the foam pieces on one side and stick them to the base. Using 8mm (⁵⁄₁₆in) staples, staple the foam in place around the edges (**G**).

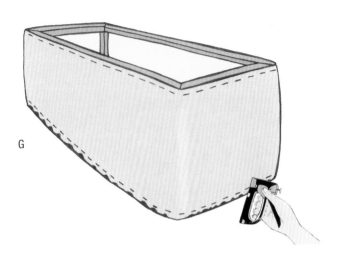

G

Tip

Don't worry about the staples compressing the foam. Once you've added the other layers you won't see the indentations.

11 Apply two layers of polyester wadding over the foam, tearing away any excess at the top or bottom edges.

12 Measure and cut a piece of calico to fit the front and sides of the base and another to fit the back. Staple in place at the back corners using 8mm (⁵⁄₁₆in) staples, and trim off any excess (**H**).

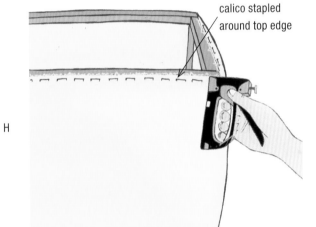

calico stapled around top edge

H

Tip

Calico doesn't fray, so you don't need to turn the edges of the calico as you staple.

13 Starting with the back of the base, measure and cut a piece of fabric to fit, allowing for a turning allowance of 3cm (1⅛in) on all sides. Turn the fabric to the wrong side and lay the top edge of the fabric along the rim of the base. Use back tack tape to attach the fabric to the top edge of the base (see Techniques: Back Tack Tape).

Tip

Use back tack tape to create a neat edge and eliminate the need to hand sew.

14 Add one layer of polyester wadding to fit over the calico on the back of the base. Fold the fabric around the sides and staple a line down the edge into the base side using 8mm (⁵⁄₁₆in) staples. This line of staples will not be visible as the front panel of fabric will cover them.

15 Measure and cut the fabric for the front and sides of the base (cut as one piece). Attach using back tack tape to the rim, as before. Snip into the corners of the fabric as you turn the corners to avoid puckering (**I**).

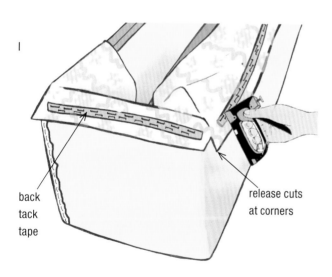

I

back tack tape

release cuts at corners

16 Add one layer of polyester wadding to fit over the calico on the sides and front of the base only. Pull fabric over and staple it to the underside of the base using 6mm (¼in) staples. Fold under the side edges and pin all the way down using small pins.

The Finishing Touches

17 Stitch the pinned edges of the lid and the base with slip stitch (see Techniques: Knots and Stitches) (**J**).

Tip

Keep the slip stitches close together for a neater look.

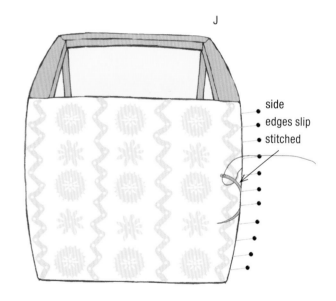

J

side edges slip stitched

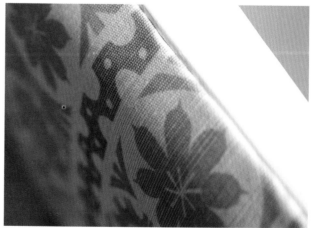

18 Measure and cut a piece of platform cloth for the underside of the base. Attach with 6mm (¼in) staples all the way around, placing the staples every 2.5cm (1in). Start in the middle of each side and work your way out to the corners, pulling taut as you go.

19 Use a quick unpick to make little slits in the platform cloth over the screw holes where the legs are attached. Screw in the legs.

20 Screw the lid to the base and start filling your finished blanket box.

ERCOL SOFA

The Ercol Windsor range was first launched in the 1950s. The strong wooden frames of these low casual sofas have stood the test of time. I love the spindle detail of the back and I think it's a real shame to cover it up, so for my reupholstery, which is done entirely on a sewing machine, I've replaced the back cushions with low rectangular ones made from vintage linen tea towels, to show off as much of the frame as possible. The back cushions are stuffed with polyester fibre, but you could try feather-filled back cushions too.

This Ercol sofa was packed with oversized cushions obscuring its beautiful frame.

NOW THE ICONIC DESIGN IS VISIBLE AND THE UPHOLSTERY HAS GONE FROM BEIGE TO BRIGHT.

Watch my time-lapse video of this project from start to finish. Scan this QR code or key the following into your browser: http://youtu.be/Kk-HCPAUUe0

Fabric Focus

Get cosy with a green textured wool, go classic with a moquette fabric, or try a colourful spin on a traditional houndstooth wool.

  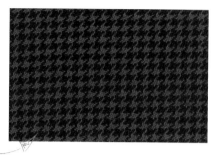

TOOLS AND MATERIALS

Basic sewing kit

Upholstery weight fabric, 3mL x 40W
(3¼ydL x 55inW)

100% linen tea towels, three unused

Stockinette, 3m (3¼yd)

56g (2oz) polyester wadding
(batting), 13mL x 67cmW
(14½ydL x 26inW)

10cm (4in) gold foam, three
pre-cut pieces measuring
67cmL x 53cmW (26inL x 20inW)
to fit Ercol shape

Cushion inners, three measuring
50cmL x 67cmW (20inL x 26inW)

Upholstery thread

Zip length, beige, 4.5m (5yd)

Zip heads, six

Notepad and pencil

Sewing machine with zip and
straight foot

Iron and ironing board

Magi mix, linseed oil or varnish
(optional)

Measuring Up

You will need just over a metre of fabric for each of the seat's box cushion covers, giving you enough spare for the backing panel of one of the back cushions too. Measure the top, bottom and borders of a box cushion and map the parts out onto a piece of paper to make a fabric cutting plan (see Techniques: Measuring and Cutting Fabric).

Stripping Down

Remove the seat cushion covers. If the foam is starting to deteriorate, have three more cut to size at your nearest foam-cutting store in either 10cm (4in) or 12.5cm (5in) foam. (The back cushions are not required as these are being replaced.)

Repairs

If the frame is worn, sand it lightly and give it another coat of varnish to deepen the colour tone. If you have a blond-wood Ercol, freshen the wood up by oiling it.

If the webbing has broken or become slack, replace it with either 50mm (2in) or 35mm (1½in) Pirelli webbing (this type of webbing is attached with a staple and plate rather than with a web stretcher).

Tip

Depending on the Ercol model, one, two or three seaters can be found, and the spindle design may vary.

RE-ASSEMBLY

Back Cushions

1 Take your inner cushion and measure it with a tape measure. Cut a piece of fabric to fit across the back of the cushion, allowing for a 1.5cm (⅝in) seam allowance. This is your backing fabric. With wrong sides facing, pin the backing fabric to one of the tea towels along the bottom edge. To ensure you have the pattern of the tea towel exactly where you want it, you may need to trim the tea towel to size before inserting the zip.

2 Using the straight foot attachment on your sewing machine, sew the two pieces together along the pinned edge, removing the pins as you sew. Press the seam open. Using the zip foot, insert a length of zip along the sewn seam (see Techniques: Putting in a Zip). Open the fabric out to the right side and use a quick unpick to unpick the closed seam where the zip lies, leaving a 1.5cm (⅝in) sewn seam at each end (**A**).

3 Open the zip a little and re-fold the fabrics so that they are right sides facing, then sew all the way around the remaining three edges. Make sure to use the backing fabric side as your guide to the 1.5cm (⅝in) seam allowance as the tea towel may end up with a larger seam, depending on its size. Trim the seams with pinking shears (**B**) before turning the cushion cover through to the right side. Insert the cushion inner and zip up. Make two more back cushions in the same way.

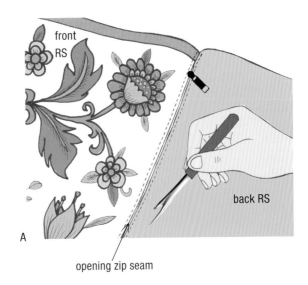

front
RS

back RS

A

opening zip seam

Seat Cushions

4 Start by covering the seat foam cushions in two layers of polyester wadding and stockinette (see Techniques: Making Up a Foam Cushion). This will make them more comfy for sitting on.

5 Make paper templates of the foam cushions: the two end cushions should be the same size and shape, while the middle cushion will be square, so you will need two templates.

6 Pin one of the templates in place on your fabric. With a ruler, mark a 1.5cm (⅝in) seam allowance all the way around the template (**C**) and cut it out around the marked line for the cushion cover top. Unpin the template, turn it over, and repeat the process for the cushion cover bottom. Place the two sides together to make sure they are a perfect fit.

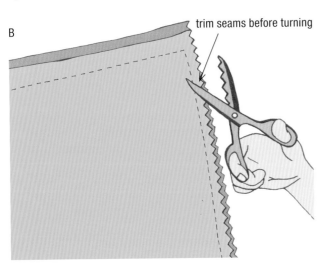

B

trim seams before turning

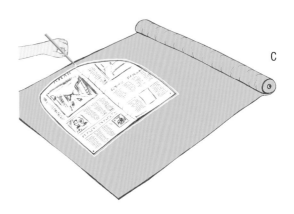

C

7 To determine the border width, measure the foam thickness with a ruler, compressing it slightly by about 1cm (⅜in). Add a 1.5cm (⅝in) seam allowance to the top and bottom and write this measurement down.

8 The box cushion border is cut into two sections: the front section 'box border' and the back section 'zip border'. Use your paper templates to determine the total length of the border by measuring all the way around the template edge. Write this measurement down. An easy way to determine the box border and zip border length is by using the working width of the fabric for the box border length, in this case 137cm (54in), then deduct this from your noted down measurement and use the remainder as the length measurement for the zip border.

9 On your fabric mark out the length and width of the box border with a straight ruler, remembering to account for a 1.5cm (⅝in) seam allowance all the way around.

10 The zip border width will be slightly wider when cut, to allow for the zip. The zip measures 3cm (1⅛in), so add this to the total width. Also add the usual 1.5cm (⅝in) to all sides of the zip border.

11 Cut the zip border as one piece, then fold it in half length ways and cut it down the middle. You are now ready to insert your zip between these two pieces (see Techniques: Putting in a Zip) (**D**).

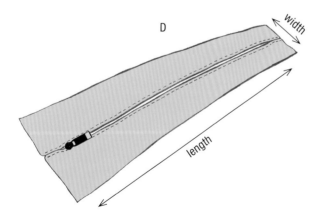

D
width
length

12 Sew the zip border length to the box border (**E**).

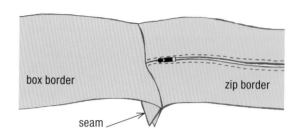

E
box border
zip border
seam

13 To sew the top and bottom of the cushion accurately to the border, a series of 'notches' are snipped into the selvedge edge. This allows you to place them together, pin and sew accurately. Start by determining the mid points of the border by folding it in half and snipping a small triangle into the seam allowance (**F**).

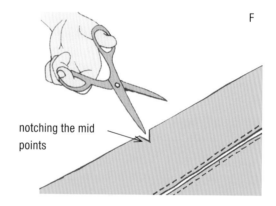

F
notching the mid points

14 The mid points of the cushion cover top and bottom are located by folding the fabric in half then into quarters and cutting small triangular notches into both the cushion cover top and bottom. With wrong side facing, pin the border to the right side of the cushion cover top exactly at the triangular snippet and continue pinning all the way around, matching the triangles (**G**).

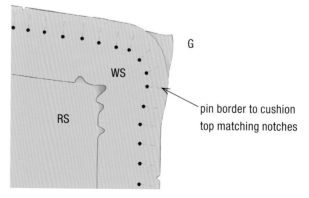

G
WS
RS
pin border to cushion top matching notches

15 Start sewing the cushion cover top to the border using straight stitch along the 1.5cm (⅝in) seam allowance. It's best to start from a mid point and work towards the corners, removing pins as you go. When you come to a corner, make some release cuts into the seam allowance to reduce puckering (**H**). Repeat this process with the cushion cover bottom. Before you start sewing, open the zip slightly to help when you come to turn the cushion cover the right way. The top and bottom cushion cover panels are cut to exactly the same size, so make sure you align them exactly before you sew the cushion cover bottom to the border.

16 When you have finished sewing, before you snip off any loose threads, check the fit. Put your hand through the zip border and turn the cushion cover the right way and pop it onto the seat cushion. If you need to make any adjustments, mark the place with a dress pin, remove the cover and adjust. Once you are confident of the fit, finish the seam edges with pinking shears (**I**) before reinserting the seat cushion.

Tip

If your fabric is particularly prone to fraying, zigzag the seam edges on the sewing machine.

H

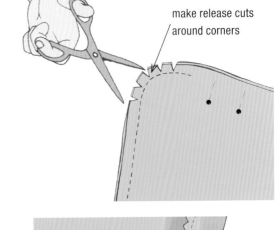

make release cuts around corners

I

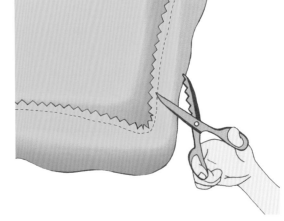

VINTAGE SEWING BOX

I just adore these 1950s sewing boxes with removable legs. You can find them in many different box shapes, leg sizes and colours. I have two filled to the brim with vintage ribbons, braiding, buttons and other crafty bits and bobs (plus the occasional toy car put there by my son). Upholstering a sewing box is quite quick and uses a relatively small amount of fabric, making it perfect for using beautiful vintage remnants. I particularly love vintage Scandinavian prints with their bright and geometric colourful patterns.

With its flimsy wicker box and frayed fabric lid, this is probably best hidden away under your hoard of fabric.

THIS BRIGHT AND CHEERY SEWING BOX WITH ITS DOMED LID AND FABRIC BASE, CAN NOW HAVE PRIDE OF PLACE IN YOUR CRAFT ROOM.

Watch my time-lapse video of this project from start to finish. Scan this QR code or key the following into your browser: http://youtu.be/Nc1J0wXHLX8

Fabric Focus

These little sewing boxes come in all styles, so too do your fabric choices, from 1950s novelty to a chirpy barkcloth, or maybe a modern atomic.

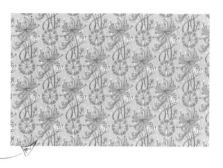

TOOLS AND MATERIALS

Basic toolkit

Basic health and safety kit

Fabric, 100cmL x120cmW
    (39inL x 47inW)

Lining fabric, 50cmL x 120cmW
    (20inL x 47inW)

Platform cloth, 30cmL x
    50cmW (12inL x 20inW)

56g (2oz) polyester wadding, 1mL x
    67cmW (39inL x 26inW)

2.5cm (1in) grey foam, one sheet
    measuring 50cm (20in) square

Thick cardboard, 45cmL x 25cmW
    (18inW x 10inL)

Size 6mm (¼in) and 8mm (⁵⁄₁₆in)
    staples, one box of each

Medium piping cord, 100cm (39in)

Back tack tape (cardboard tack
    strip), 100cm (39in)

Ribbon, 25cmL x 1cmW
    (10inL x ⅜inW)

Upholstery thread, 50m (54yd)

Decorative tacks, four

Spray glue

Notepad and pencil

Wood filler (optional)

Magi mix, linseed oil or varnish
    (optional)

Spray paint for legs (optional)

Measuring Up

Take measurements for the box across the top of the lid, around three sides of the base (one piece), and the back section of the base. The inside of the base is lined, so also take measurements for the inside lid, all four sides and across the bottom. Remember to add turning allowances to your measurements.

It's best to wait until you have covered the lid and base with calico before you cut the fabric, particularly if you choose a fabric with a pattern. I like to place the fabric onto the lid first and to measure the base pattern lines from there. (For further information on measuring, see Techniques: Measuring and Cutting Fabric.)

Stripping Down

Use a staple or tack remover, mallet and pliers to remove all the plastic wicker, plastic edging, foam and fabric from the outside of the box and the lining from the inside: you may need to cut the wicker to remove it. Don't panic about the flimsy looking frame: it will be reinforced by the layers as you build the new upholstery. Dispose of all the old materials. Remove the lid by unscrewing the hinges from the box base, but leave the hinges attached to the lid. Put the screws in a safe place.

Repairs

The wooden tapered legs on these sewing boxes are either black, white or natural wood. If there are lots of scuffs, gently sand down and re-apply paint. To restore natural wood legs, oil with linseed oil.

Tip

Have a pair of scissors handy when stripping down your sewing box.

RE-ASSEMBLY

Lid Section

1 To make a domed seat for your sewing box, cut a small rectangular piece of 2.5cm (1in) foam to fit in the centre of the lid about 10cm (4in) from the edge in all directions. Spray glue one side of the foam in a well-ventilated area, leave for 30 seconds to go tacky, then stick it to the top of the lid (**A**).

2 Cut another piece of 2.5cm (1in) foam to fit exactly to the edge of the lid. Spray glue on one side and stick down over the smaller piece of foam. Trim any excess from the sides (**B**).

3 Cover the foam with two layers of polyester wadding across the top and down the sides of the lid. Pinch the wadding together at the corners and trim off any excess from the underside of the lid.

4 Measure across the top of the lid to the underside and cut a piece of calico to fit. Lay the calico on your table and place the lid on top, foam side facing down. Starting at the middle of each edge, staple the calico to the underside of the lid using 6mm (¼in) staples making sure to cut around the hinge holes using a 'V' cut (see Techniques: Fabric Cuts and Pleats). At each corner make a bed sheet pleat (see Techniques: Fabric Cuts and Pleats) (**C**).

A

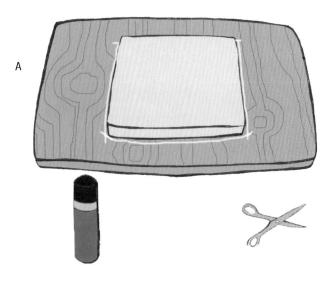

B

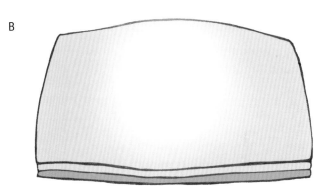

5 Turn the lid top-side up and apply one layer of polyester wadding over the calico, making sure that any excess wadding is removed.

6 Lay your top fabric over the lid to see where you want to apply the pattern, and mark with chalk.

calico stapled to underside

C

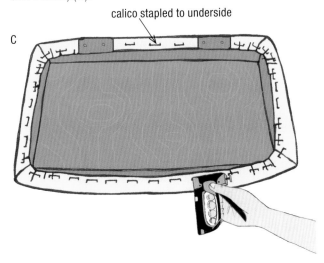

Tip
Make sure you have the pattern flowing down the sewing box – don't just cut from the selvedge.

7 Staple the fabric to the underside of the lid using 6mm (¼in) staples as with the calico (see step 4). Trim off any excess fabric and calico around the staples.

8 Now measure the circumference of the lid and make some single piping, one longer length and one to fit between the hinges, following Techniques: Single and Double Piping.

9 Attach the longer length of piping first, using 8mm (⁵⁄₁₆in) staples, and working from the mid point of the piping to attach it to the front of the lid. Continue to staple the piping around the lid to the hinges – your piping should just peek over the edge of the lid, but none of the selvedge should show. When you reach the hinges, snip off any excess piping cord, fold the ends of the fabric in and staple to secure.

Tip
You may need to snip a release cut as you take the piping around the corners.

10 You can now screw the hinges back in. Apply the shorter length of piping between the hinges in the same way, making sure you do not cover the hinges.

11 Now apply the lining to the inside of the lid. Start by measuring and cutting a small piece of calico to fit inside the lid; staple it in place around the edges close to the piping using 6mm (¼in) staples, and then trim off any excess.

12 Cut the lining fabric to size. leaving a 1.5cm (⅝in) turning allowance on each side. Turn the lining to the wrong side and attach it along the top edge using back tack tape, cutting the tape to fit between the hinges (see Techniques: Back Tack Tape) (**D**).

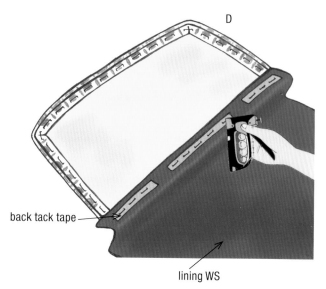

D

back tack tape

lining WS

13 Add one layer of polyester wadding up to the piping, then fold the fabric over the wadding (the fabric will hide the hinge plates). Turn the fabric under at the edges and pin along the piping line all the way around (**E**).

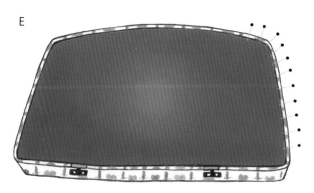

E

Base Section

14 Cut a piece of calico to fit around the outside of the frame of the base. Staple the calico in place using 6mm (¼in) staples (**F**). Trim off any excess calico close to the staples.

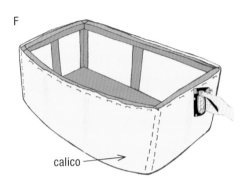

calico

15 Measure and cut the fabric for the outside of the base. The fabric will be cut in two sections: one to fit around the front and sides and the other to fit across the back. When planning for the cutting of your fabric, try to get the pattern on the base to line up with the pattern on the lid when closed. Remember to allow for the turning allowances to fix the fabric over the top edge of the box and underneath the base.

16 Add one layer of wadding over the calico on the front and sides allowing it to fold over the top edge and trimming it at the bottom edge. Attach the top edge of your fabric to the inside of the box and the bottom edge to the underside (**G**). Start stapling from the middle of the front of the box and make a small pleat to fold the fabric around the corners. Staple the sides to the back of the box. These will be covered by the back panel of fabric. Trim off any excess fabric.

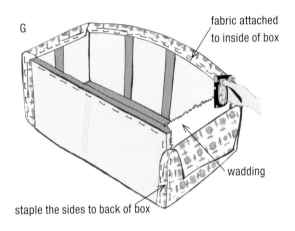

fabric attached to inside of box

wadding

staple the sides to back of box

17 Now measure, cut and staple the fabric for the back panel. Staple the top and bottom edges in the same way as the front panel. Fold under the side edges and pin along the corner edge (**H**).

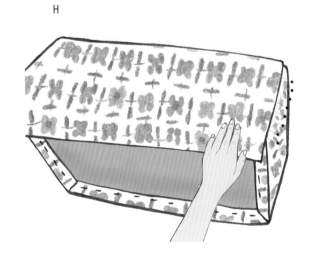

18 To line the base, start by adding some pieces of wadding to fit the spaces of the inner frame (**I**).

19 The fabric for the lining is measured and cut in three sections: the front and sides (cut as one piece), the back and the base. Attach the front/sides piece first. Use back tack tape to attach the lining fabric to the top edge of the frame (see Techniques: Back Tack Tape) (**I**); fold the fabric over to the inside of the box, pull it taut and staple it to the base. Use back tack tape to attach the back piece of lining fabric, fold the fabric to the inside of the box, fold under the side edges, pull the fabric taut and staple it to the base (**J**).

20 Make a paper template to fit the base of the box and use to cut out a piece of thick cardboard to fit. Spray glue the underside of the cardboard base insert, place a piece of polyester wadding on top and wrap with the lining fabric, and stick the fabric in place on the underside (**K**). Push the covered insert into the base of the box.

I

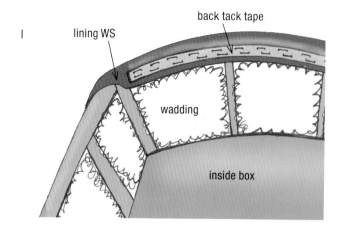

back tack tape

lining WS

wadding

inside box

J

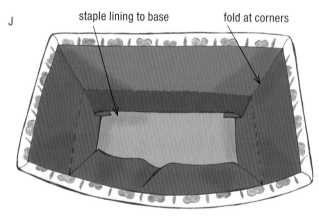

staple lining to base

fold at corners

K

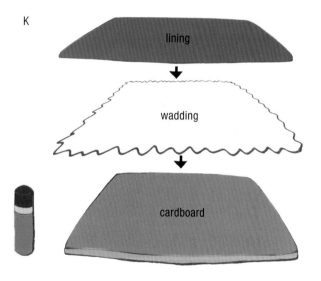

lining

wadding

cardboard

The Finishing Touches

21 Sew the pinned areas of the base and the lid using slip stitch (see Techniques: Knots and Stitches).

22 Turn the box upside down and cut a piece of platform cloth to fit the base. Fold the edges under and staple in place using 6mm (¼in) staples. Screw in the legs: to allow the screws to pierce through the fabric without it buckling, snip a small cross over each hole with a quick unpick.

23 Turn the box upright and re-attach the lid. Add a piece of canvas ribbon to each side to hold the lid up when the box is open. Determine the length required and cut two pieces. Use decorative tacks to attach the ribbon to the inside edge of the lid and the inside edge of the base.

FLUTED HEADBOARD

This DIY headboard can be sized to the width you want. Lengths of cut foam are applied to a chipboard base, and each flute is individually upholstered, so you could mix and match the fabric for a patchwork effect. The finished headboard is attached to some bed legs and its taller than average height will make it a real focal point for your bedroom. Or, if you prefer, you may be able to find a pre-made headboard to cover. The bed legs can be purchased separately, or you can attach it directly to the wall.

The headboard is easy to assemble from pre-cut foam, pre-cut chipboard and bed brackets.

THIS RIPPLED FLUTED HEADBOARD MAKES A REAL STATEMENT PIECE FOR YOUR BEDROOM.

Watch my time-lapse video of this project from start to finish. Scan this QR code or key the following into your browser. http://youtu.be/T1Szyk7r4ro

Fabric Focus

Luxuriate in a cotton velvet, create a vintage patchwork or use a beautiful neutral linen to let your bedding do the talking.

  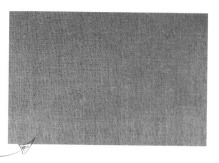

TOOLS AND MATERIALS

Basic toolkit

Basic health and safety kit

Upholstery weight fabric, 3mL x 140cmW (3¼ydL x 55inW)

Fire-retardant calico, eight strips measuring 120cmL x 20cmW (47inL x 8inW) and two strips measuring 120cmL x 25cmW (47inL x 10inW)

56g (2oz) polyester wadding (batting), 10mL x 67cmW (11ydL x 26inW)

5cm (2in) blue foam, 10 pieces pre-cut to 115cmL x 15.5cmW (45inL x 6inW)

Size 8mm (⁵⁄₁₆in) staples, one box

1.5cm (⅝in) chipboard, pre-cut to 110cmL x 160cmW (43inL x 63inW)

Hardwood bed legs, two 60cm (24in) high

Notepad and pencil

Drill (optional)

Measuring Up

The measurements given in the Tools and Materials list are provided as a guide. You'll need to measure your bed to determine what size board you require. The chipboard needs to be cut to the width of the mattress with at least an extra 10cm (4in) to each side.

Once you have your chipboard cut to size, decide how many foam flutes you want. Taking a couple of centimetres (an inch) off the width, divide the board up by how many flutes you require: I used 10 flutes. The extra length allows you to fold the foam at the top of the board and you can trim off any excess.

For the fabric, measure the length of the board and work out how much fabric you need for the width of each flute: if you have a patterned fabric, allow for pattern matching. I centred the pattern to the middle of the flute and my headboard used 3m (3¼yd) in total.

Tip

Have your foam for the flutes cut a little longer than needed – you can always trim them back.

Preparation

Start by marking up the chipboard. On the back, use a pencil to mark out the bed legs to match where they fit on your bed base. Drill holes for the brackets where necessary.

On the front, mark out the positions of the flutes. If your board is 160cm (63in) wide and you are using 10 flutes, divide the width of the board by 10 to determine the width of your flute channels. (Note: the flutes will have been cut to a slightly narrower width to allow for stapling.) Start by marking out the middle channel and work outwards from there to ensure symmetry.

Pre-cut all the calico and fabric strips to cover the foam flutes, making sure you leave an allowance for stapling. Note: the calico and the fabric for the end flutes will be a little wider to allow for them to be attached to the back of the board.

Place the board on a table so that the top edge (the side with the foam overhang) is positioned off the edge of the table during the upholstery process.

If you intend to wall mount the headboard, prepare the brackets on your wall first and mark out the bracket location on the back of the chipboard.

ASSEMBLY

The Flute Channels

Note: each individual flute is upholstered to top fabric in succession. When spray gluing the foam flutes, work in a well-ventilated area; spray one side only and leave for 30 seconds to go tacky before fixing in place on the chipboard.

1 Start by spray gluing the first piece of foam, then attach it to one of the middle channels marked on the board, lining the edge of the foam up to the bottom edge of the board. The top of the flute will overhang at the top edge of the chipboard (**A**).

2 Place two layers of polyester wadding over the top of the flute (do not extend the wadding down the sides of the flute). Place a strip of calico on top and staple in place all the way along one side using 8mm (⁵⁄₁₆in) staples, pulling the calico taut over the flute, then stapling along the other side. Stop stapling about 5cm (2in) from the top and bottom and leave the top and bottom edges open for now (**B**).

3 Where the foam overhangs at the top of the board, use a bread knife to cut a 1cm (³⁄₈in) deep channel into the back of the foam flute (**C**). This will allow you to fold the foam to the back of the board easily.

4 Pull the foam overhang to the back of the board and staple in place to create a nicely rounded shape (**D**). Trim off the excess foam. Leave the top and bottom edges of the calico unattached at this point.

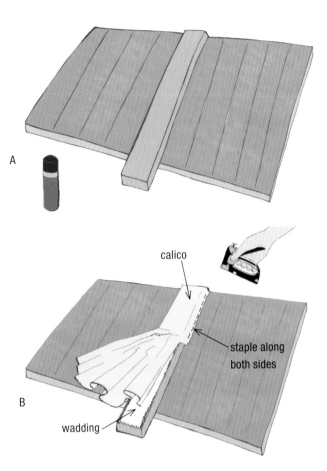

A

calico

staple along both sides

wadding

B

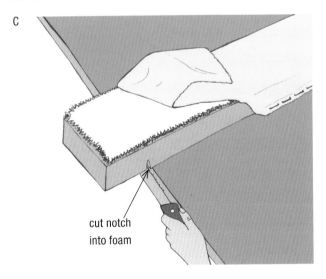

C

cut notch into foam

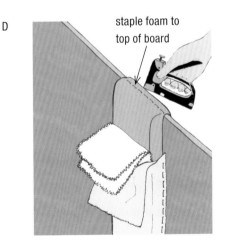

D

staple foam to top of board

Tip

You can choose to staple the top of the foam as you place each flute onto the board, or leave until you have fixed all the flutes in place.

5 Add one more layer of polyester wadding to the top of the flute (as in step 2) then cover with one of your pre-cut top fabric strips, stapling all along one side, then the other, leaving the ends unstapled (**E**).

6 You are now ready to add the next flute, and all additional flutes will be added in the same way. Take a strip of top fabric and with wrong side facing up lay it over the covered flute. Staple the fabric along its edge, over the covered flute's existing staples and as close to the foam as possible without pinching it. Now staple the calico strip along the same edge as the top fabric strip.

7 Spray glue your next piece of foam and stick it in place close up to the first flute (**F**). Cover the top of the flute with two layers of polyester wadding.

8 Take the strip of calico over the foam flute (leave the top fabric strip for now), pull it taut and staple it along the edge of the newly inserted foam flute. (If you are stapling the top of each foam flute into place on the back of the board as you go, do so now (steps 3 and 4.) Add one layer of polyester wadding to the top of the flute (**G**). Now you can pull the top fabric across and staple it along the same edge as the calico strip.

9 Repeat step 8 until you reach the end flute at either side. For the end flutes, you'll need to attach the calico and top fabric to the back of the chipboard. You'll also need to make sure your polyester wadding forms over the top of the flute and all the way down the side edge of the chipboard. Pull the chipboard to the edge of the table to enable you to crouch down underneath to staple it in place. Do not be tempted to staple up towards you as this might result in a nasty accident. Note: you may need to trim off some of the flute along this edge with a bread knife.

E
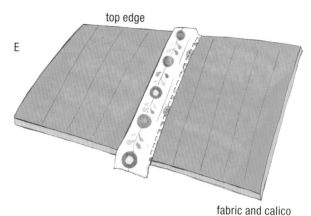
top edge

F
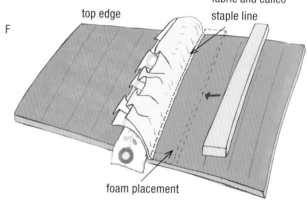
top edge

fabric and calico staple line

foam placement

G
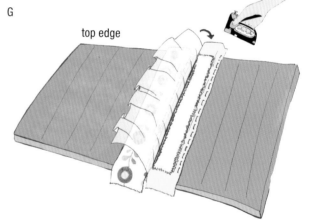
top edge

The Finishing Touches

10 You can now pleat and staple the top and bottom edges (it doesn't matter if you start at the top or the bottom of the headboard). Pull the headboard to standing position on a clean sheet on the floor (to avoid getting your fabric dirty). First staple the calico and then the top fabric onto the back of the chipboard, folding it under at each side to form a neat edge on each flute (**H**). Repeat the process at the other end of the headboard.

11 Lay a sheet on your table then place the headboard face down on top. Cut a piece of platform cloth or calico to fit the back and staple it in place using 8mm (5⁄16in) staples, folding the edges under as you go.

12 Finally, screw the bed legs in at the marked out location at the base of the headboard and attach to the bed base.

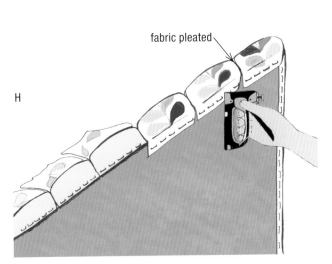

fabric pleated

H

ROUND BEDROOM CHAIR

If you are looking for a small dressing table chair, then a 1960s Sherborne is a perfect fit. The rounded shape is formed by a plywood structure, which was built for occasional use rather than for comfort, so I've re-padded the seat with a nice thick foam as well as adding caster wheels to gain a little height. I've chosen a bold pattern with a strong geometric print, and combined it with a luxurious velvet for the seat. I have removed the original button detail around the base and some purple velvet piping to highlight the chair's curves.

With its gold satin fabric and synthetic braiding, this small bedroom chair is stuck in the 1960s and needs sprucing up.

NOW VIBRANT AND BOLD, WITH NEW CASTER WHEELS, THIS DRESSING TABLE CHAIR IS BOTH FANCY AND FUNCTIONAL.

Watch my time-lapse video of this project from start to finish. Scan this QR code or key the following into your browser: http://youtu.be/xLymsxzh8zY

Fabric Focus

Go all out for pattern with a vivid print, tone it down with a geometric design, or choose a luxurious vibrant pink velvet.

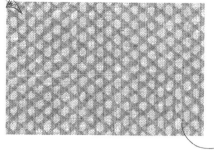

TOOLS AND MATERIALS

Basic toolkit

Basic health and safety kit

Upholstery weight fabric, 150cmL x 140cmW (59inL x 55inW)

Fire-retardant calico, 1mL x 150cmW (39inL x 59inW)

Platform cloth, 100cm (39in) square

56g (2oz) polyester wadding (batting), 3mL x 67cmW (3¼ydL x 26inW)

2.5cm (1in) grey foam, one sheet measuring 50cm (20in) square

1.25cm (½in) blue foam, one sheet measuring 100cm (39in) square

Size 6mm (¼in), 8mm (⁵⁄₁₆in) and 10mm (³⁄₈in) staples, one box each

Medium piping cord, 2.5m (2¾yd)

Upholstery thread

Button twine, 2m (2⅛yd)

Carpet thread (waxed thread), 3.5m (4yd)

Large button back, one

Spray glue

Notepad and pencil

Caster wheels, four (optional)

Wood filler (optional)

Measuring Up

This is a small chair, so you won't need to buy masses of fabric. Take your tape measure and measure up the chair. I upholstered it in three sections (inside back, seat front, and outside back) and I used a different fabric for the seat itself. Write your measurements down on a piece of paper and use them to make a fabric cutting plan (see Techniques: Measuring and Cutting Fabric).

Stripping Down

Remove the steel-capped feet with a staple remover, then take off the platform cloth from the base. Start removing the fabric from the bottom up using a staple or tack remover and mallet. Dispose of the materials but keep the thin plywood piece that the seat cushion was resting on.

Repairs

There were no repairs needed on this frame, although you may find that you have to fill the plywood where the feet where hammered in if there are large holes (see Techniques: Stripping and Filling). As this chair is made in one piece and fully upholstered, any significant damage to the plywood would probably render it unusable.

Tip

The feet could be replaced with either wheel casters or new wooden bun feet.

RE-ASSEMBLY

Base

1 Start by measuring the areas you are going to cover with the 1.25cm (½in) foam, which is everywhere except the seat. I cut my foam in three sections: outside back, seat front and inside back. Make a template of each section and cut the foam to size.

2 Working in a well-ventilated area, spray glue the foam pieces on one side, then stick each piece to the chair; reinforce each section by stapling it with 8mm (⁵⁄₁₆in) staples all the way around (**A**). Trim any foam at the edges of the chair.

3 Cover the foam-covered sections with two layers of polyester wadding (**B**).

4 Next add the calico. It's easier to make a slip cover to fit over the chair. First cut two pieces of calico to fit over the inside back and the outside back, and pin together with wrong sides facing. Machine stitch together using straight stitch leaving a 1.5cm (⅝in) seam all the way around, finishing your stitching a couple of centimetres (inch or so) away from the seat edge. Turn the calico to the right side and slip over the chair back. Staple in place using 8mm (⁵⁄₁₆in) staples.

5 Cut a piece of calico to fit around the seat front and staple in place using 8mm (⁵⁄₁₆in) staples, folding the edges where they meet the calico on the seat back (**C**).

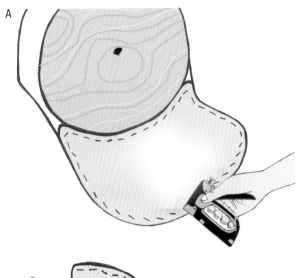

A

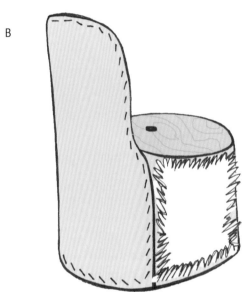

B

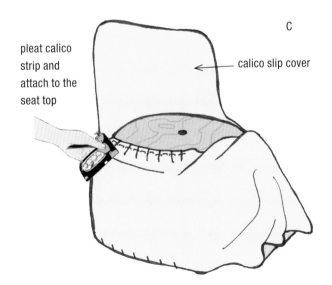

pleat calico strip and attach to the seat top

calico slip cover

C

Adding Fabric

6 Cut a piece of fabric to fit the inside back. Make sure you measure around the seat curve where the seat widens. You want your fabric to be symmetrical down the chair, so use your eye to determine the mid point and mark it with a pin. The fabric will be attached to the outside back and seat base so allow for an extra turning allowance of about 3cm (1⅛in) on each edge.

7 Add one layer of polyester wadding to the inside back, then staple your fabric in place using 8mm (⁵⁄₁₆in) staples, aligning the mid point of the fabric to the mid point of the outside back. Start to staple from the top of the chair working your way down the outside back: you will need to make some release cuts to ensure the fabric doesn't pucker (**D**). Alternate your staples around the back edge with those stapled to the back of the seat edge, so you keep the fabric nice and taut.

8 Next cut your fabric for the seat front: this will end where you determine the back of the chair starts, so mark this up on the foam first before measuring for the fabric. Try to make the fabric symmetrical to that on the inside back, making sure the mid point of the seat front fabric is the same as the mid point of the inside back fabric and that the pattern matches.

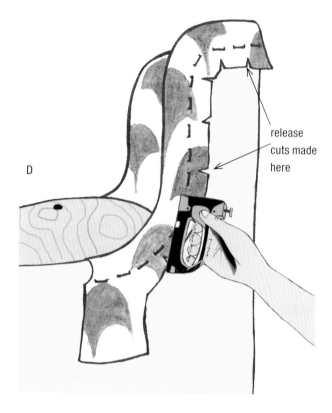

D

release cuts made here

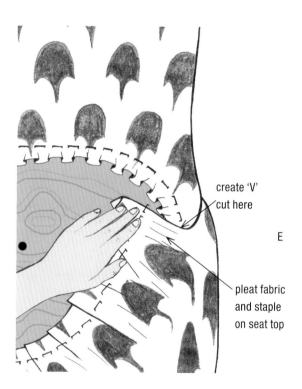

create 'V' cut here

E

pleat fabric and staple on seat top

9 Starting at the mid point of the seat front, staple the fabric to the seat using 8mm (⁵⁄₁₆in) staples, and alternate with stapling the fabric to the underside of the chair. Keep the fabric taut at all times to avoid significant puckering around the base edge. As you attach the fabric to the seat, you will need to make folds in the fabric, but make sure these don't show on the visible part of the seat front (**E**). Where the seat front fabric meets the inside back, make a small 'V' cut at each side to fold under the excess fabric and staple down (see Techniques: Fabric Cuts and Pleats).

10 Measure how much piping is needed to go around the back of the chair. Cut your fabric and sew the single piping to length following Techniques: Single and Double Piping. Attach the piping in one strip to the back and side edges along the staple line where the fabric ends.

11 Measure and cut the fabric for the outer back section making sure that the pattern lines up with the inside back and seat front sections. Add one layer of polyester wadding to the outer back. Pin the fabric in place, turning it under at the edges and pinning it to the piping as you go along. At the bottom edge, staple the fabric to the underside of the chair with 6mm (¼in) staples: make sure you smooth it with your hand as you attach it to avoid puckers and make any pleats required underneath the chair so that they do not show.

Seat

12 Now to make the seat. Take the thin plywood base and draw around it onto a piece of 2.5cm (1in) grey foam, and cut out. Spray glue the back of the foam in a well-ventilated area and stick it to the plywood base. Cover the top of the foam with two layers of polyester wadding.

F

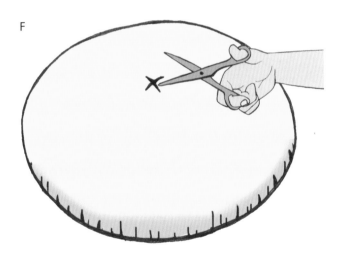

13 Cut a piece of calico to fit around the seat and staple it to the underside using 6mm (¼in) staples. Find the hole in the middle of the seat top and push a skewer through it. Mark the point with a black cross and remove the skewer. Cut the cross (**F**) and remove some of the wadding beneath the hole.

14 Now measure the seat for fabric cutting: you will need a circular piece for the seat top, a border piece measured to the circumference of the seat and wide enough to be attached to the seat's underside, and single piping for the top edge (full circumference) and bottom edge (part circumference to inside back).

15 Make pieces of single piping: one piece to fit the circumference of the seat at the top edge and one piece for the bottom edge, ending at the inside back (see Techniques: Single and Double Piping).

16 Take your piece of border fabric and sew the short ends together. Sew the long piping length to the top edge of the border using the piping foot. Next pin the circular top piece into the border with wrong sides facing and sew all the way around.

17 Cover the seat with another layer of polyester wadding, tearing off any excess from the underside. Slip the cover over the seat and attach it to the underside (plywood base) using 6mm (¼in) staples.

18 Now to add the remaining piece of piping to the underside of the seat. Place the seat upside down on the chair and chalk on the underside the points where the seat hits the inside back of the chair. Staple the piping from chalk mark to chalk mark. When you get to the end, cut away any excess piping cord, tuck in the ends of the fabric and staple in place (**G**).

19 Cover the underside of the seat with platform cloth, stapling it in place with size 6mm (¼in) staples.

20 Next make your button for the middle of the seat cushion (see Techniques: Buttons). To attach the seat to the base, thread a button needle with the button twine from the button and push it through the middle of the seat cushion, out the other side and through the hole in the base (**H**). Pull the cushion taut to the seat and staple the button twine in a zigzag fashion to the underside of the chair using 8mm (⁵⁄₁₆in) staples.

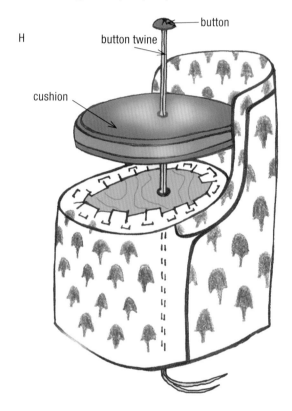

H

button

button twine

cushion

G

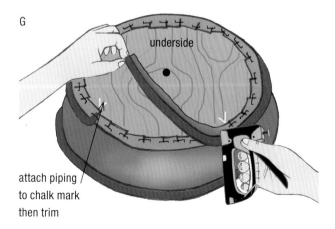

underside

attach piping to chalk mark then trim

The Finishing Touches

21 Use slip stitch to sew the outside back fabric along the piping line, removing the pins as you go (see Techniques: Knots and Stitches) (I).

22 Cut a piece of platform cloth to the shape of the base of the chair, with a turning allowance 1.5cm. (0.6in). Using size 6mm (¼in) staples and folding the edges under as you go, staple the platform cloth to the underside.

23 Find the raised areas on the base where the feet should be located. Cut a little hole through the platform cloth to allow the screws to go through the fabric easily and screw four small caster feet into place.

Tip

You may need to pre-drill the holes for the caster wheels.

I

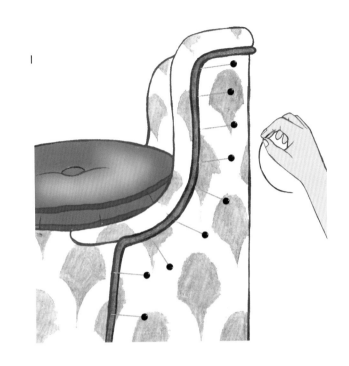

BUTTONED FOOTSTOOL

Deep buttoning is a skill that requires

precision and practise, but there is a slightly

easier way to achieve it, by placing each

piece of fabric onto the furniture separately

and adding a button to each individually.

This is a great method if you want to create

a patchwork effect using a variety of fabrics.

I've cut up a piece of vintage barkcloth into

squares and placed them side by side to

create a unique design.

This faux leather footstool has been machine sewn as one piece to create a buttoned look and is very uninspiring.

EACH INDIVIDUAL PIECE OF FABRIC HAS BEEN PLACED
AND HAND SEWN TO CREATE A UNIQUE PATTERN TOP
TO THIS MID-CENTURY FOOTSTOOL.

Watch my time-lapse video of this project from start to finish. Scan this QR code or key the following into your browser: http://youtu.be/WlatBY5m3e0

Fabric Focus

Choose a cosy tartan and try alternating lines, or try a thick weave in shocking pink, or go bold with a modern print.

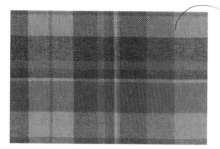  

TOOLS AND MATERIALS

Basic toolkit

Fabric, 100cmL x 120cmW
(39inL x 47inW)

Fire-retardant calico 60cmL x 75cmW
(23inL x 29inW)

Platform cloth, 45cmL x 60cmW
(17inL x 23inW)

56g (2oz) polyester wadding (batting),
150cmL x 67cmW (59inL x 26inW)

10cm (4in) grey foam, pre-cut to
45cmL x 60cmW (17inL x 23inW)

Size 6mm (¼in) and 8mm (⁵⁄₁₆in)
staples, one box each

Carpet thread (waxed thread),
3m (3¼yd)

Button twine, 6m (6½yd)

Fabric-covered loop back
buttons, 12

Spray glue

Drill

Iron and ironing board

Notepad and pencil

Magi mix, linseed oil or varnish
(optional)

Wood filler (optional)

Measuring Up

If you're using a plain fabric, this size of footstool shouldn't need more than 50cm (20in) of fabric. If you want to place the fabric into a design like mine, pulling out details of the pattern, then you may need a little more material.

When measuring up for the individually placed squares, you need to allow for a turning allowance on each side, but the size will depend on the square's attachment position (see Adding Fabric).

Stripping Down

Low 1960s footstools like this one tend to have been stapled and made as a unit, so they are very quick to take apart. Start by unscrewing the legs and put them to one side. Remove the platform cloth and take out the staples from the faux leather. The buttons may be stapled to the base with twine and if so, be sure to remove this too. At this point you

should be able to lift off the foam and faux leather fabric to dispose of it.

If you want to add buttons to a footstool that doesn't already have them, simply mark out the holes on the base of the webbing once you have applied it, alternatively if the footstool has a plywood base, drill holes in the formation you want, then add the rest of the layers as described in the re-assembly steps.

Repairs

If necessary, re-drill the holes in the footstool's plywood base. On occasion I have stripped the footstool to find the plywood has a crack in it, and if this has happened it's best to get a new piece cut to size; you should be able to unscrew the leg brackets to re-use them. Rub the legs of the footstool down with some white spirit (mineral spirits) to clean them or give them a fresh coat of paint – the legs would have been painted black originally.

RE-ASSEMBLY

Footstool

1 Start by placing your 10cm (4in) foam onto the plywood base. If it's not an exact fit, trim it with a bread knife. Spray glue the foam on one side in a well-ventilated area and stick it to the base (**A**).

2 Add two layers of polyester wadding to fit over the top and sides of the footstool. Pinch the wadding together at the corners to reduce bulk and trim off any excess to the underside.

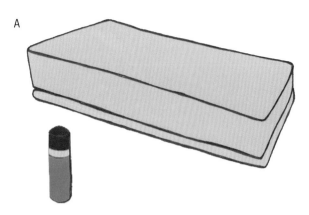

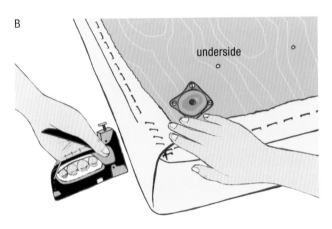

3 Measure across the top of the footstool to the underside and cut some calico to fit, allowing for a turning allowance. Lay the calico on your table and place the footstool on top, covered side facing down. Starting at the middle of each edge, staple the calico in place using 6mm (¼in) staples. Pull the calico taut but not so tight that it buckles. Fold the corners with a bed sheet pleat (see Techniques: Fabric Cuts and Pleats) (**B**).

Tip

If the calico has been pulled too tight, creating lumps, remove the staples one at a time and re-apply.

4 Mark out the placement for your buttons on the top of the footstool by piercing skewers through the foam. Use a pen to mark a cross at each skewer before removing, then snip the lines of the cross (**C**). Remove some of the wadding beneath each cross.

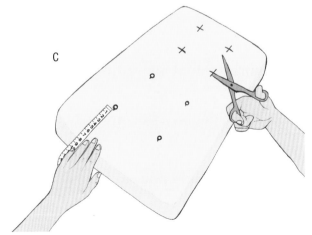

Adding Fabric

5 In order to cut the fabric, start by working out how many squares of fabric you need. The turning allowance is determined by where the individual square is placed on the foostool as follows:

Middle squares: 3cm (1⅛in) all around;

Edge squares: 12.5cm (5in) on one side and 3cm (1⅛in) on the other three sides;

Corner squares: 12.5cm (5in) on two sides and 3cm (1⅛in) on two sides.

You can either cut all the squares at the start or do it as you go along, building up the pattern as you go. The squares need to be added to the footstool in a certain order to make sure the pleats all go in the right direction. Use the grid (**D**) to order your squares.

layout for fabric squares

D

15	11	13	12	14
5	1	3	2	4
10	6	8	7	9

6 Start by placing a piece of polyester wadding in square 1, making sure you cut it exactly to the square size with no turning allowance. Place a middle fabric square over the wadding and skewer each corner in place through to the holes in the plywood base (**E**).

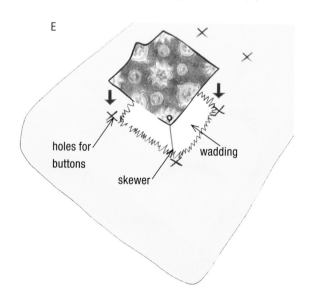

E

holes for buttons

skewer

wadding

7 To attach the fabric square, tack each corner in place: take a button needle threaded with carpet thread through each corner and attach the thread to the underside of the plywood base using a zigzag method, stapling it in place in one direction, then pulling and stapling it in another direction (see diagram (**G**). Remove each skewer as you go. Repeat process for square 2.

8 With square 3, add a piece of wadding to fit the square, then fold the side edges of the fabric using the turning allowance guidance in step 5. Skewer the corners and tack in place as before. The top and bottom edges are not folded (**F**).

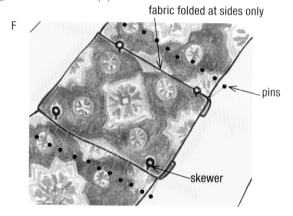

fabric folded at sides only

F

pins

skewer

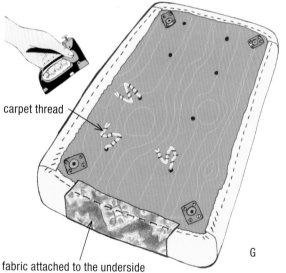

carpet thread

fabric attached to the underside

G

9 Place squares 4 and 5 over the wadding, folding the edge that falls over the previously placed square. Skewer the corners into the holes and pull the opposite side of the fabric around to the underside of the footstool and staple it in place with 6mm (¼in) staples (**G**).

10 Continue to add the squares in the layout shown in (**D**), making sure to fold whenever the fabric square falls over another piece of fabric and to staple onto the underside where the fabric square falls over the side.

11 For the corner squares, create a bed sheet pleat (see Techniques: Fabric Cuts and Pleats (**H**).

Adding Buttons

12 When you have attached all the squares of fabric, you can add the buttons. To add the buttons, thread the loop with button twine and thread onto a button needle. Push the needle through the hole, securing with a strip of calico and an upholstery knot on the underside (see Techniques: Buttons). Pull the buttons fairly taut: they should depress the foam a little when attached.

H
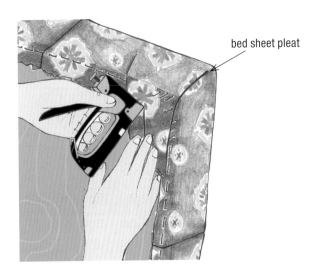
bed sheet pleat

The Finishing Touches

13 Cut a piece of platform cloth to fit the underside of the footstool and allow for a turning allowance. Using size 8mm (⁵⁄₁₆in) staples and folding the edges under as you go, staple the platform cloth in place; start from the middle of each edge and pull the cloth taut as you work.

14 Screw the legs back onto the base of the footstool, cutting a little hole in the platform cloth with a quick unpick so the fabric doesn't pucker.

Tip
Keep any bits of scrap calico – they come in handy when adding buttons.

PATCHWORK NURSERY CHAIR

If you are looking for a small piece of furniture for a bedroom or playroom, these vintage 1950s boudoir chairs are the perfect starter project. The frames are solid wood and well built, plus the round base will usually be constructed with a spring mesh unit so you don't need to worry about attaching springs yourself. I've used a yummy 1960s vintage curtain for the main seat and some new cotton-based fabric for the arms and back. Detailed with single piping and chrome decorative tacks, this is the perfect little person chair.

The dreary fabric and the exposed lumbar support made this little chair look very dated.

THE DRAYLON HAS BEEN REMOVED AND THE ARMS HAVE BEEN RE-SHAPED. THIS BRIGHT PLAYFUL AND STURDY CHAIR WILL BE PERFECT FOR A CORNER IN A PLAYROOM.

Watch my time-lapse video of this project from start to finish. Scan this QR code or key the following into your browser: http://youtu.be/W0q2aiV6m-0

Fabric Focus

Choose a floral pattern for a perfect fit in a bedroom corner, try a London scene for a little boy's room or opt for an abstract cotton print in navy, turquoise and black.

  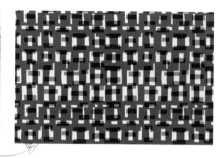

TOOLS AND MATERIALS

Basic toolkit

Basic health and safety kit

Upholstery weight fabric,
 3mL x 140cmW (3½ydL x 55inW)

Fire-retardant calico,
 150cm (59in) square

340g (12oz) hessian (burlap),
 100cm (39in) square

Platform cloth, 100cm (39in) square

56g (2oz) polyester wadding
 (batting), 8mL x 67cmW
 (8¾ydL x 26inW)

2.5cm (1in) grey foam, two sheets
 measuring 100cm (39in) square

1.25cm (½in) blue foam, one sheet
 measuring 100cm (39in) square

Size 6mm (¼in), 8mm (⁵⁄₁₆in) and
 10mm (³⁄₈in) staples, one box each

Jute webbing, 6m (6½yd)

Medium piping cord, 3m (3½yd)

Laid cord, 2m (2¼yd)

Back tack tape (cardboard tack strip),
 150cm (59in)

Upholstery thread

Carpet thread, 4m (4½yd)

Cord twine no.4, 4m (4½yd)

16i tacks, 25g (1oz)

Silver decorative tacks, 50

Spray glue

Notepad and pencil

Wood filler (optional)

Measuring Up

Before you begin to strip down the chair, measure the chair. This will allow you to determine how much fabric you will need to buy for your project. If you were using a plain fabric you would need 2.25m (7ft 4in) (see the example cutting plan in Techniques: Measuring and Cutting Fabric); however, as I used three different fabrics for a patchwork effect, more fabric was required.

Stripping Down

Start by removing the platform cloth from the bottom of the chair with either a tack or staple remover and mallet, pulling out any staples left behind with some pliers. Then take the outside back panel and outside arm panels off. Next take off the seat top, inside arms and inside back removing and disposing of all fabric, stuffing and hessian as you go.

Tip
You might find a pair of strong scissors also useful for the stripping down stage.

Repairs

Every piece of furniture will vary on how much cosmetic and structural repair is needed. Often, it isn't until you have stripped the chair back to its frame that you can accurately identify any structural problems, but if there are any little wobbles, not to worry, most things can be sorted with a bit of wood glue and a G-clamp.

Any deep holes left in the framework caused by removing the tacks, can be filled using wood filler made using a mixture of wood glue and sawdust to fill the holes (see Techniques: Stripping and Filling).

Tip
Tired legs can be sanded and re-varnished or oiled for an extra lease of life.

RE-ASSEMBLY

Seat Base

1 Secure the movement in the seat by zigzagging some laid cord around the front section of the spring mesh unit (between the chair arms). Measure this section and double it; this is the length of laid cord you will need. Partly hammer in the 16i tacks so that they are about half way in and approximately 10–15cm (4–6in) apart around the front section of the chair frame.

2 Starting from the first tack on the left, wrap the laid cord around it leaving about 10cm (4in) length loose on one end. With the longer end, feed the cord through the front edge of the spring mesh unit and back down, pulling the laid cord taut, but not so hard that it pulls the spring mesh unit forward. Wrap the cord around the next tack and repeat this all the way around the front of the seat, hammering down the tacks as you go. Finish by tying the two loose ends to the nearest spring using a cow hitch (see Techniques: Knots and Stitches). Trim any excess laid cord (**A**).

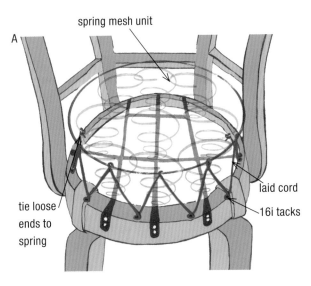

spring mesh unit

A

tie loose ends to spring

laid cord

16i tacks

3 Measure across and down the sides of the spring mesh unit to the wooden frame. Add a 3cm (1⅛in) turning allowance to each side and cut the hessian to the measured size. Pull the hessian taut over the unit, turning the edges back on themselves to avoid fraying, and start to staple into position around the top edge of the frame using 10mm (⅜in) staples.

4 Start by stapling the mid points and leave the areas around the legs and arms until last. You will have to put pleats into the hessian as it falls around the circular shape to get a tight fit. Make some cuts around the arms of the chair and staple down (see Techniques: Fabric Cuts and Pleats).

5 Use twine to blanket stitch all the way around the top of the spring mesh unit to secure the hessian in place (**B**) (see Techniques: Knots and Stitches).

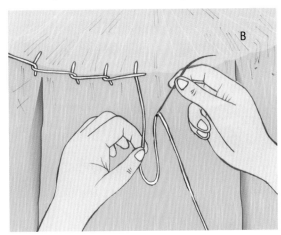

B

Inside Back and Inside arms

6 Start by adding strips of webbing to the inside of the frame. This chair used two pieces of webbing on the inside back and two on each arm. If your frame is wider, you may need more. Using a web stretcher to attach the webbing to the inside of the frame, attach the webbing to the back and arm rail (see Techniques: Webbing and Tack Roll) (**C**).

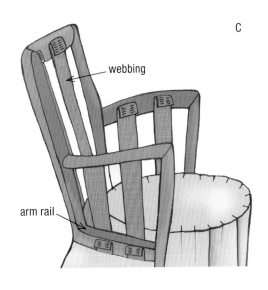

C

webbing

arm rail

7 Cut three pieces of hessian to fit the inside back and each of the inside arms. Add a 3cm (1⅛in) turning allowance to your measurements. Take the inside back piece and fold the hessian edges inwards by the turning allowance; using 8mm (⁵⁄₁₆in) staples, start stapling the hessian to the inside back frame, working outwards from the middle and leaving the bottom edge unstapled. Now staple hessian pieces to the inside arms, again starting form the middle, but this time leave both the back edge and the bottom edge unstapled. Take the unstapled edges under the arm and back rails and use skewers to pin them out of the way for now (**D**).

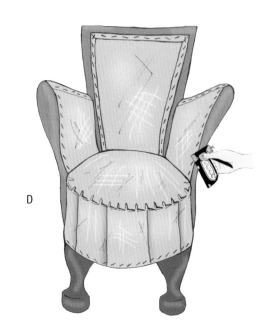

D

8 Cut a lumbar support from 1.25cm (½in) foam. This should be a half-moon shape measuring the width of the inside back and about 30cm (12in) high. To attach, spray glue the back of the foam and place at the base of the hessian, just above the seat (**E**).

E

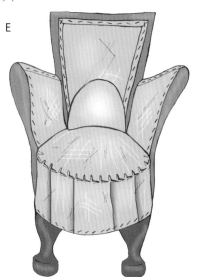

9 Make a template of the inside back panel of your chair and use it to cut a piece of 2.5cm (1in) foam. Attach the foam in place along the front edges of the frame using spray glue, then staple with 10mm (⅜in) staples (**F**). Repeat this process with a layer of 1.25cm (½in) foam to establish the desired thickness of the inside back.

F

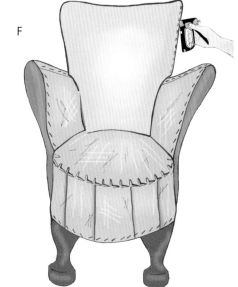

10 Cover the foam with two layers of polyester wadding making sure it doesn't creep over the back edges of the frame. At the corners pinch to pull out any excess bulkiness.

Tip

The wadding should stick to the foam without the need of glue or stapling.

Tip

Trim the foam around the edges with scissors or a bread knife so it doesn't produce unwanted bulkiness when you come to add the fabric.

11 Measure over the foam to the outside edges and to the bottom edge of the frame and cut a piece of calico to fit. Attach the calico using 6mm (¼in) staples to the outside frame. Attach two or three staples to the mid points of t he top and sides and staple towards the corners, keeping the calico taut as you go. You will need to make some cuts around the arm rails and bed sheet pleats at the top corners (see Techniques: Fabric Cuts and Pleats) (**G**).

12 Make a template of the inside arms and cut two 2.5cm (1in) foam pieces to fit. The foam should come to the edge of the frame but not across the front edge of the arm. Use spray glue to attach and reinforce with size 10mm (⅜in) staples around the edge of the frame (**H**).

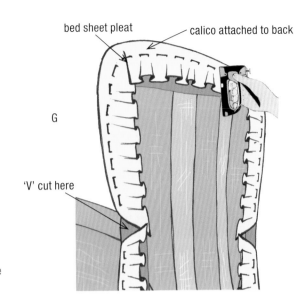

bed sheet pleat

calico attached to back

G

'V' cut here

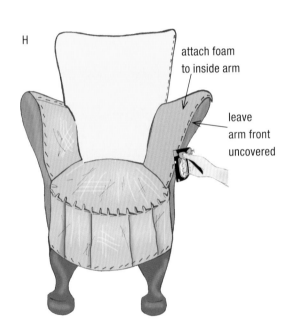

H

attach foam to inside arm

leave arm front uncovered

13 Add two layers of polyester wadding to the arms. Take the polyester wadding all the way across the front edge of the arm (where there is no foam) and rip it off around the edge of the frame.

14 Measure the inside arms taking the tape measure from the top outside edge of the frame, all the way to the bottom outside edge of the frame, and for the width, from the back all the way across the front of the arm panel. Cut two pieces of calico and use 6mm (¼in) staples to attach in place, making the necessary cuts in the calico around the frame (see Techniques: Fabric Cuts and Pleats) and leaving the back edge and bottom edge unstapled. Take the calico under the bars and pin as you did with the hessian.

Tip

Excess wadding that peeks over the edges can easily be ripped to the desired size.

Seat Top and Front

15 Make a template of the top of the seat to cut your foam to size. Use two layers of 2.5cm (1in) foam, cutting one layer to the template and another roughly half that size. Spray the smaller piece of foam with glue and place it in the middle of the seat. Spray the larger piece of foam and cover the smaller piece – doing this creates a nice dome effect. For the panel at the seat front, cut and staple one layer of 1.25cm (½in) foam (**I**).

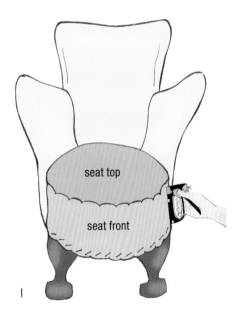

seat top

seat front

I

16 Cut and add two layers of polyester wadding over the seat top and the front edge. Wadding does not have to be added to the back or sides of the seat as these will be enclosed by the arms and inside back of the chair.

17 Add calico to the seat by sewing a slip cover. This reduces the need to pleat the calico around the seat base. Measure the seat top, taking the tape measure to the outside edges and under the frame. Measure for a separate piece of calico across the front panel to the underside. Mark the seat top calico around the front edge with a pencil to show the curve and pin the front panel to it, leaving a 1.5cm (⅝in) seam allowance. Machine stitch using straight stitch.

Tip

To reduce puckering around the front edge, snip some release cuts in the seam allowance of both layers of calico.

18 Attach the calico slip cover using 8mm (⁵⁄₁₆in) staples. The calico will be attached under the arm and back rails at the back, and to the underside of the frame at the front and along the arm fronts. Start by adding a couple of staples to the middle of each section of the chair. You will need to make cuts around the frame at the front and back of the seat (see Techniques: Fabric Cuts and Pleats). Trim off any excess calico (**J**).

19 Add another layer of polyester wadding over the calico on the seat, arms and inside back of chair.

Adding Fabric

20 Starting with the inside back, take your chosen upholstery fabric and spend some time working out where you want the pattern to fall before cutting. Place the fabric over the inside back of the chair and pin around the frame edge to create a cut line making sure to leave the usual turning allowance, then cut the fabric using your cutting plan as a guide (see Techniques: Measuring and Cutting Fabric).

21 Staple the inside back fabric to the outside part of the frame top and sides and leave the bottom edge loose (as with the calico and the hessian). Cut release cuts around the arms as you staple down the frame, but leave the top corners until last, then fold neatly with a bed sheet pleat and staple into position (see Techniques: Fabric Cuts and Pleats) (**K**).

22 Similar to the calico, the seat is sewn separately, but with the addition of single piping. You want the seat fabric to match the line of the pattern flowing down the chair from the inside back, so pop the fabric onto the seat top and mark the mid pattern point with a pin. Measure the seat top and sides, as with the calico, and the front panel as a separate piece, and cut the fabric. This time, pin a line around the front seat curve and on the reverse of the fabric draw a sewing line with chalk or a pencil (**L**).

K

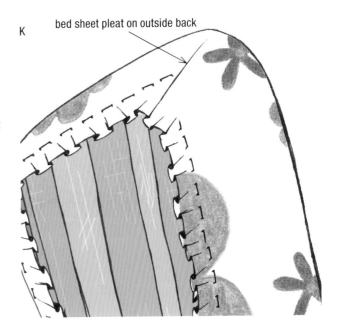

bed sheet pleat on outside back

L

pinned line

23 Make single piping (see Techniques: Single and Double Piping) and attach it by sewing it to the top of the front seat panel. Make some release cuts every 1cm (⅜in) along the piping selvedge.

24 Using the chalked line on the seat top fabric as a guide, pin the front panel, wrong side, to the seat top, wrong side. Machine stitch using straight stitch and a piping foot. Turn the seat fabric the right way and attach to the frame using 10mm (⅜in) staples, as with the calico, making the necessary cuts around the frame, including the front legs (see Techniques: Fabric Cuts and Pleats).

25 Measure and cut the fabric to fit the inside arms. As with the calico, the arm fabric is attached to the outside of the frame. Start by stapling the middle top edge, but this time staple the bottom edge to the frame. Make the necessary cuts needed around the frame and work your way up to the arm corner. Make a bed sheet pleat and attach to the back of the arm.

26 Once all the fabric on the inside of the chair is attached, it's time to attend to the layers that you pinned up out of the way. Remove the skewers and staple each layer down, one by one, using 10mm (⅜in) staples. Trim off any excess fabric.

Tip

If you are using a patterned fabric, try to match your pattern on the seat to the inside back panel pattern for a nice finish.

The Finishing Touches

27 Add a line of decorative tacks to the fabric around the legs at the front of the chair. Fold the fabric under and add individual tacks close to each other using a magnetic tack hammer.

Tip

To soften the blow, wrap the tip of your magnetic tack hammer with a piece of wadding and cover with calico to gently knock in decorative tacks.

28 Now make some single piping to attach to the top edge of each of the arms and the outside back. To attach the piping to the frame, start by folding the excess under the bottom of the chair frame, then work your way up along the outside edge of the arm stapling 10mm (⅜in) staples into the piping selvedge as you go. At the corner, make a release cut to avoid puckering, then carry on to the end, snipping off any excess. Repeat for the other arm and for the outside back edge. The outside back piping should finish at the arm top.

29 Next cut some calico to fit the outside sections of the arms and back. The calico should fit into the frame section and be attached using 8mm (⁵⁄₁₆in) staples all the way around (**M**).

Tip

If the selvedge of the piping is adding too much bulk at the corners, snip release cuts into the selvedge.

30 Measure and cut the fabric for the outside arms and outside back panel making sure you have a turning allowance around each edge.

31 Start by attaching the outside arm fabric. At the top edge of the fabric add a length of back tack tape to the reverse along the piping edge, and staple in using 10mm (⅜in) staples (see Techniques: Back Tack Tape). Add a piece of wadding to cover the calico and pull the fabric taut back over the wadding and calico to attach to the underside and outside back edge of the chair using 10mm (⅜in) staples. Pin the fabric along the piping line at the front edge using dress pins (**N**). Repeat this process for the other arm.

M

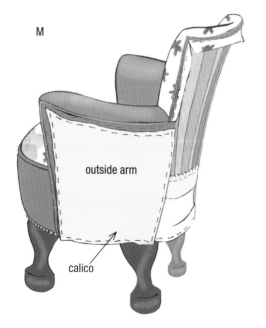

outside arm

calico

N

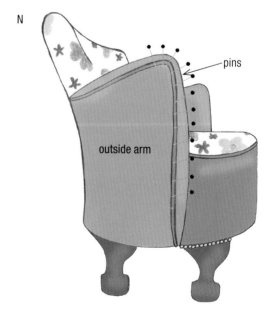

pins

outside arm

Tip

To attach your outside back fabric along a
straight line, use a metre ruler (yardstick) and
chalk to draw a faint line to work along.

32 To attach the outside back fabric, use back tack tape along
the top edge as before, add a layer of wadding and fold the
fabric back over, attaching it to the underside of the frame.
Fold and pin the sides, first down the piping edge and then
in a straight line to the bottom edge.

33 Sew all the pinned edges using slip stitch (**O**)
(see Techniques: Knots and Stitches).

34 Finally, turn the chair over, measure and cut some platform
cloth to fit, then staple to the bottom of the frame to hide all
of the loose threads. Cut around the legs as needed (see
Techniques: Fabric Cuts and Pleats).

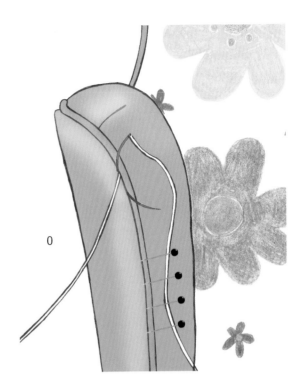

MID-CENTURY SOFA

I love slender furniture from the 1950s and 1960s. A statement piece, such as this Parker Knoll, was designed with upright elegance in mind in contrast to today's slouch couch. The back and seat are made from one piece of foam so this sofa is fairly easy to assemble. The key to this style is slimline so make sure you don't overstuff the arms. I have covered the sofa in a beautiful textured fabric and attached buttons to add detail to the inner back. The fabric has been railroaded to avoid having to join it across the outside back and to limit the overall amount of material needed.

This mid-century sofa has excellent bone structure, but with its drab beige upholstery fabric, it is in need of a dramatic transformation.

THE MUSTARD-COLOURED, TWISTED WOOL FABRIC AND BUTTON DETAIL HAS BROUGHT THIS ELEGANT PIECE RIGHT UP TO DATE.

Watch my time-lapse video of this project from start to finish. Scan this QR code or key the following into your browser: http://youtu.be/tYXMxPvm5FU

Fabric Focus

Go darker with a teal wool or smooth and silky with a soft textured blue, or use a pretty geometric print all over.

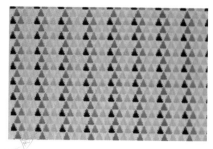

TOOLS AND MATERIALS

Basic toolkit

Basic health and safety kit

Upholstery weight fabric, 6mL x 140cmW (6½ydL x 55inW)

Fire-retardant calico, 3mL x 150cmW (118inL x 59inW)

340g (12oz) hessian (burlap), 4m (4⅜yd)

56g (2oz) polyester wadding batting), 20mL x 67cmW (21ydL x 26inW)

5cm (2in) blue or grey foam, two sheets pre-cut to 65cmL x 160cmW (25inL x 62inW)

1.25cm (½in) blue foam, one sheet measuring 2m (2⅛yd) square

2.5cm (1in) grey foam, one sheet measuring 100cm (39in) square

Size 6mm (¼in), 8mm (⁵⁄₁₆in) and 10mm (⅜in) staples, one box each

Jute webbing, 2m (2⅛yd) on the roll

Back tack tape (cardboard tack strip), 4m (4⅜yd)

Medium piping cord, 6m (6½yd)

Button twine, 2m (2⅛yd)

Carpet thread (waxed thread), 5m (5½yd)

Upholstery thread

Large button backs, four

Notepad and pencil

Spray glue

Varnish (optional)

Measuring Up

When you get your mid-century sofa home, your first job is to take the measurements of all the parts, as outlined in Techniques: Measuring and Cutting Fabric. Once you've created your fabric cutting plan, you can start searching for the perfect fabric. If you choose a pattern, make sure the fabric can be railroaded to avoid the need to seam it.

Stripping Down

The stuffing may well have started to crumble, so have protective glasses and a mask close to hand. Using a tack or staple remover and mallet, start to remove the fabric from the base of the sofa. The sofa is fairly cumbersome to move about, so turn it onto its outside back and, kneeling on the floor, gradually unpick the fabric attached to the base. Use pliers to remove the remaining staples or tacks then turn the sofa back onto its legs and start taking off the back panels from the arms and back.

Tackle the inside areas last: gradually unpeel the layers and dispose of the contents as you go. The wings will need to be unscrewed: put these to one side and keep the screws safe.

The arm section is taken off from the outside first. This sofa has wooden arm caps that can be lifted off with a staple remover and mallet – just be careful not to damage the wood.

Tip

At the stripping down stage I make a note of the foam thickness to check that what I put back in will create the same shape.

Repairs

This sofa is fitted with tension springs, which eliminated the need to web the bottom or the back, but in similar pieces you may have to web the base with jute or herringbone webbing. If your sofa has tension springs, check that they are taut; if they have started to sag, they will need replacing. Tension springs can be bought individually.

If the wooden arm caps and legs are dull, wipe with magi mix. Alternatively, give them a light sanding down and re-apply varnish.

RE-ASSEMBLY

Arms Section

1 Start by adding a strip of webbing to each arm to create an arm roll. Using 10mm (⅜in), staples attach the webbing to the front inside arm and, using a web stretcher, pull across to the outside back of the arm (see Techniques: Webbing and Tack Roll for how to apply). The location of the webbing should be around 5cm (2in) above the seat frame (**A**).

2 Measure and cut two pieces of hessian to fit the inside arms, allowing for a 3cm (1⅛in) turning allowance all the way around. Starting from the middle of the arm, staple the hessian using 8mm (⁵⁄₁₆in) staples making sure you fold over the edges to avoid fraying. Leave the back and bottom edge unattached but pin it up with a skewer out of the way for now (**B**).

3 Add foam to the arms. Start by measuring and cutting 1.25cm (½in) blue foam to fit the front and inside part of the arm; a template may be useful here. Then add a layer of 2.5cm (1in) foam to cover the arm top, leaving space for the wooden arm cap. Spray glue on one side and staple the foam in place using 10mm (⅜in) staples. Don't staple the back edge or bottom edge of the inside arm foam (**C**). Use a bread knife or scissors to trim off any excess foam.

Tip

Line the bottom edge of the foam on the front arm with the seat edge.

A

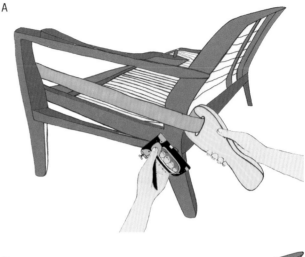

B

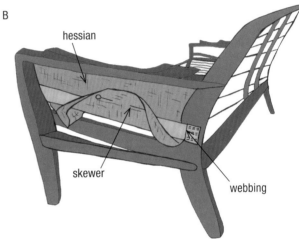

hessian

skewer

webbing

C

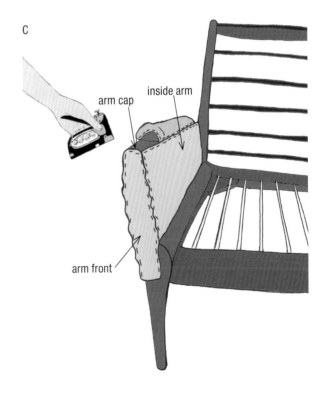

arm cap

inside arm

arm front

4 Cover the foam with two layers of polyester wadding making sure to trim any excess.

5 Measure the arm and cut pieces of calico to fit over the inside and front edge of the arm making release cuts as necessary to fit it around the frame (see Techniques: Fabric Cuts and Pleats). The front edge will need a 'V' cut so the fabric fits under the arm and around the front arm edge, and the back of the arm will require a straight cut. Cut a section out of the top edge where the arm cap fits and staple the calico to the frame using size 6mm (¼in) staples (**D**).

Tip

The calico for the arm is cut as one piece and sweeps around the front arm.

Seat Section

6 Measure and cut a piece of hessian to fit over the seat to cover the tension springs, allowing for a turning allowance of 3cm (1⅛in) all the way around. The back edge will be pulled through to the back. Starting from the middle front edge, attach the hessian using size 8mm (⁵⁄₁₆in) staples (**E**). At the back edge make 'V' cuts to fit the hessian around the frame, pull it through to the outside back and attach with staples.

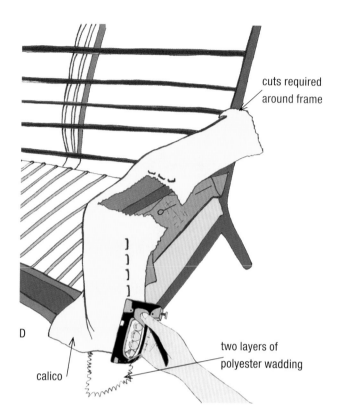

D

cuts required around frame

two layers of polyester wadding

calico

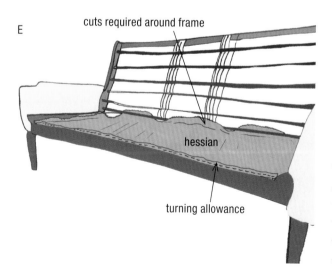

E

cuts required around frame

hessian

turning allowance

7 When you are attaching large pieces of foam, like the 5cm (2in) blue or grey foam for the seat and the inside back, it is much easier to get these pieces pre-cut to your exact measurements. The mid-century sofa foam is angled at the bottom of the inside back and the back of the seat so that they slot together easily. This allows you to pull your layers through to attach them to the back of the frame. Take the pre-cut foam piece for the seat and, working in a well-ventilated area, spray glue the back of it; leave for 30 seconds for the glue to go tacky, then position it on the seat so it sits right at the front edge of the seat frame, but not over it.

8 To create a rounded look to the seat edge, measure and cut a piece of 1.25cm (½in) blue foam to fit across the top and down the front edge of the 5cm (2in) foam seat base. Spray glue and attach it to the front edge of the frame using 10mm (⅜in) staples to fix it along the bottom edge of the 5cm (2in) foam: trim off overhang (**F**).

9 Add two layers of polyester wadding to exactly fit over the seat foam, tearing away any excess from the edges.

10 Measure and cut a piece of calico to fit over the seat foam. Start by attaching the calico along the front seat edge under the lip of foam, and in the middle of the back edge. As you staple along, you will need to make some straight cuts (**G**) and 'V' cuts around the frame at the back and sides (see Techniques: Fabric Cuts and Pleats). At the sides, the calico will be pulled under the arm foam and attached to the outside part of the arm frame. When you have stapled the seat calico, trim off any excess (**H**).

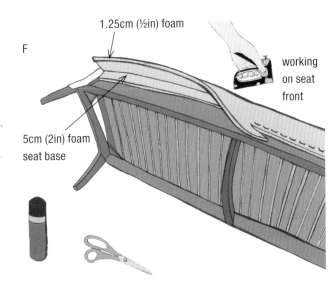

F

1.25cm (½in) foam

working on seat front

5cm (2in) foam seat base

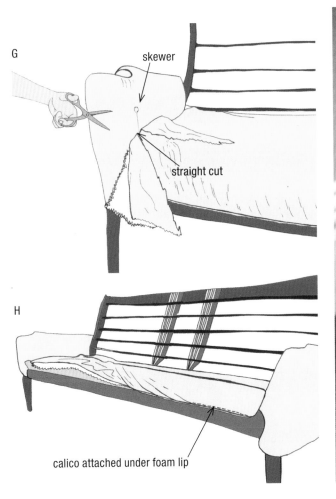

G

skewer

straight cut

H

calico attached under foam lip

Inside Back Section

11 Measure and cut a piece of hessian to fit to the inside back frame, allowing for a turning allowance (see step 2). Using 8mm (⁵⁄₁₆in) staples attach the hessian to the inside back frame, leaving the bottom edge open (**I**). Make two 'V' cuts around the middle frame bars to fit; push the bottom edge of the hessian through to tuck up at the back with a skewer.

12 Working in a well-ventilated area, spray glue the underside of the inside back piece of 5cm (2in) pre-cut foam, leave for 30 seconds for the glue to go tacky, then position it over the hessian. Press down the top edge and fix in place with a few temporary staples to allow you to trim off the foam extending beyond the top edge (**J**).

13 Add two layers of polyester wadding to the inside back but don't go over the edge of the foam, and trim or tear away any excess.

14 Measure and cut a piece of calico to fit over the inside back allowing enough seam for attaching it to the back of the frame, around 5–10cm (2–4in).

15 Start by stapling the calico at the top and bottom edge in the middle of the frame to get the calico nice and taut. Staple along the top edge, depressing the foam as you go. At the bottom edge, apply some staples to temporarily hold the calico in place – we will be removing these later, so don't use too many. Make some release cuts around the frame to fit. At the sides, make sure no foam or wadding falls into the area where the wings will be attached. Pull the calico taut and attach it close to the edge, making sure not to go over the screw holes. Make the relevant cuts required around the frame here.

16 When you staple the top corners, you can either create a bed sheet pleat as outlined in Techniques: Fabric Cuts and Pleats, or pull the calico taut to mould it around the corner, making sure the pleats are present on the back edge only.

17 Remove the temporary staples from the bottom edge and push the calico through to the back and pin it up with the other layers. Trim off any excess calico around the other edges.

I

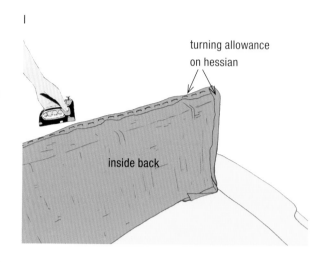

turning allowance on hessian

inside back

Tip

If your staple gun isn't up to the job, press the foam down with one hand and trim it with the other hand.

J

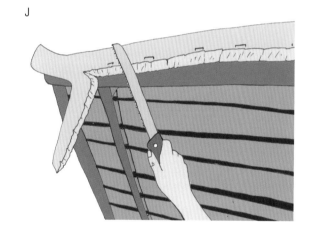

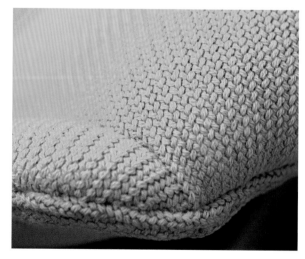

Wing Sections

18 Draw around the front of the wings onto 1.25cm (½in) foam, allowing for access to the screw holes to enable you to re-attach them later. Cut out the foam shapes, spray glue them on the reverse side, and attach to the front section of each wing. Staple around the edge using 8mm (⁵⁄₁₆in) staples (**K**).

19 Add a couple of layers of polyester wadding directly over the foam area, and then cover with calico, attaching it to the back of the wing using 6mm (¼in) staples. Trim any excess calico.

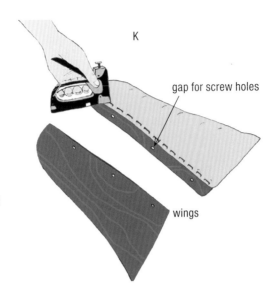

K

gap for screw holes

wings

Adding Fabric

20 Using your fabric cutting plan (see Techniques: Measuring and Cutting Fabric), measure and cut each section of fabric for the sofa and cut the piping strips.

Seat Section

21 Add one layer of polyester wadding over the seat section, tearing and trimming any excess. Then attach the fabric using 10mm (⅜in) staples. Attach a couple of staples in the middle at the sides, then start stapling from the middle of the front and back edges, working outwards and following the cutting advice in step 22. Work your way across the front edge, directly under the seat lip and all the way to the sides (**L**).

L

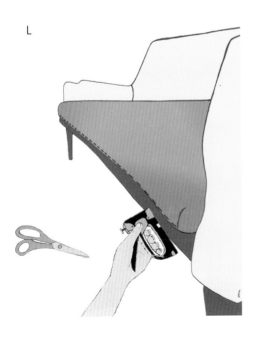

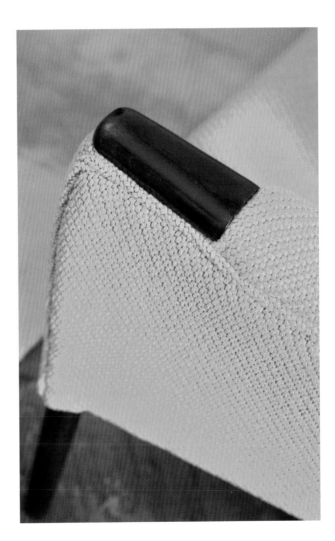

22 When attaching the fabric to the seat section, you will need to make two 'V' cuts around the back of the seat. The front of the seat, where it meets the arms, should be cut with a straight cut as in step 10, then fold the fabric under into a pleat on the front edge. The back corner by the legs also requires a 'V' cut. Once the seat fabric is securely attached, trim off any excess fabric (**M**).

M

Tip

For a neat invisible fold at the front of your seat edge, sew the pleat with slip stitch (see Techniques: Knots and Stitches).

Inside Back Section

23 Add one layer of polyester wadding over the inside back, making sure you don't cover the sides where the wings will be fitted. Trim off any excess wadding.

24 Place your fabric over the inside back and tack a few staples into each middle section of each side at the back of the frame, pulling taut as you go. Work your way along the outside back adding 10mm (⅜in) staples to both the top and bottom edge, and making cuts around the frame where necessary – see step 15, but this time the staples you place at the bottom of the frame will be permanently attached.

N

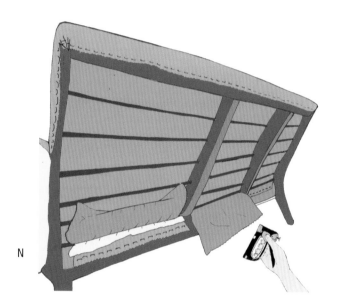

25 At the corners, pull the fabric taut and staple so you have a flat curve with no visible pleats.

26 Pull down the pinned-up layers from the back of the frame and staple them down over the fabric layer using 10mm (⅜in) staples (**N**).

27 Make and attach four buttons (see Techniques: Buttons). Mark the position of the buttons on the front of the sofa by eye, placing skewers. Then measure the distance between the skewers to make sure they are evenly spaced and adjust if necessary. Apply the buttons with button twine and staple the twine securely in a zigzag formation onto the exposed frame on the outside back using 6mm (¼in) staples.

Tip

Make sure your button twine is long enough to secure the buttons to the outside back frame.

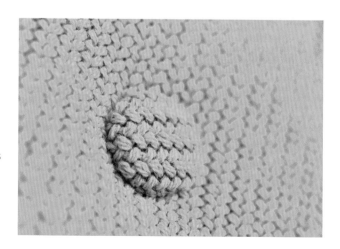

Inside Arm Section

28 Add one layer of polyester wadding over the calico on the inside arm, trimming away any excess. Place the fabric over the arm and start to staple from the middle alternating between the top and bottom inside edges of the frame and using 10mm (⅜in) staples. You will have to make some cuts around the frame – see step 5. Once the fabric is stapled, remove the skewer holding up the other layers and staple down, again using 10mm (⅜in) staples. Trim off any excess fabric (**O**).

Wing Sections

29 Add one layer of polyester wadding to the inside of the wing sections. Then attach the fabric to the front of the wings stapling it onto the outside part of the wing using 8mm (⁵⁄₁₆in) staples and allowing a gap for the screw holes.

30 Screw the covered wing sections back into the sofa frame. If there is a gap between the top of the arm and the bottom of the wing, peel back the arm fabric and add extra wadding to pad this. You are looking for a seamless line hitting the bottom of the wing.

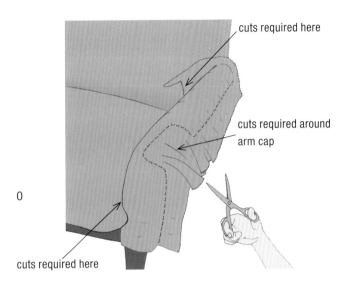

O

cuts required here

cuts required around arm cap

cuts required here

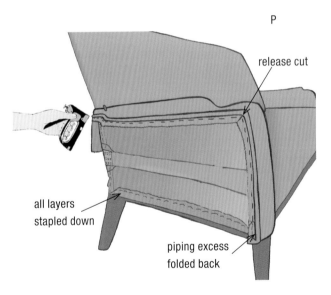

P

release cut

all layers stapled down

piping excess folded back

Tip

Staple all inside fabric parts from seat, arms and back within the sofa frame to avoid bulkiness when adding outside fabric.

The Finishing Touches
Adding Piping

31 Now its time to add piping to the outside sections of the sofa. If you haven't already done so, sew single piping using your sewing machine and a piping foot – see Techniques: Single and Double Piping. I used three separate piping pieces, two for each arm and one long length for the wings and outside back.

32 Start by attaching the piping at the bottom edge of the outside arm on one side. Leave an overhang of 2.5cm (1in) before stapling the piping in place using 10mm (⅜in) staples, working your way up and around the outside of the arms, then across under the wing to the outside back. Keep feeling the edges of the frame line with your finger and thumb to determine the placement of the cord (**P**). Repeat on the other side.

33 Take a final length of piping from the bottom edge of the wing, and up and around the wing and onto the outside back edge, all the way along to the bottom edge of the wing on the other side.

34 At the front edge on each side, tuck the excess piping up and away out of view. Unpick and remove some of the piping cord from the fabric, turn the edges under and staple down.

Front Seat Border

35 Staple a thin strip of fabric under the seat lip using back tack tape (see Techniques: Back Tack Tape) (**Q**). There is no platform cloth on this sofa, so fold the fabric under before stapling it to the underside to make a neat edge that won't fray.

Outside Sections

36 Measure and cut a piece of calico to exactly fit the shape of the outside arms and attach using 6mm (¼in) staples. Trim off any excess.

37 Add one layer of polyester wadding to fit the outside wing exactly. Place the outside wing fabric and use skewers to pin around the edges, folding the fabric under neatly up to the edge of the piping. Staple to the frame down the back edge using size 10mm (⅜in) staples (**R**).

38 Now move on to the outside arm below the wing. Apply one layer of polyester wadding to cover the calico, then use skewers to pin the outside arm fabric along the piping edge, folding the fabric under. You may need to put in a couple of staples on the back edge of the frame as you skewer. Pull the fabric to the underside of the sofa, fold the edges under and staple down using 10mm (⅜in) staples. You will need to make some 'V' cuts so the fabric fits neatly around the legs (see Techniques: Fabric Cuts and Pleats). You can now tap the wooden arm cap back onto the arm top (**S**).

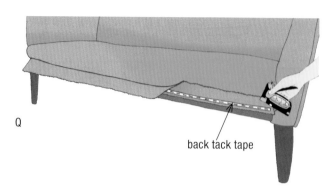

Q

back tack tape

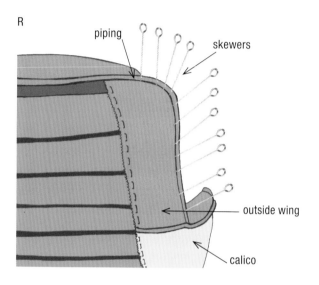

R

piping

skewers

outside wing

calico

Tip

To attach the fabric to the underside of the arms, tip the sofa onto its back.

39 Measure and cut a piece of calico to fit the outside back of the chair and staple it in place all the way around the edge. Add a piece of polyester wadding over the calico.

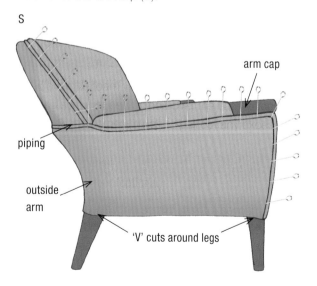

S

arm cap

piping

outside arm

'V' cuts around legs

Tip
To keep the wadding in place, pin it to the frame with skewers and remove the pins as you add the fabric.

40 Using back tack tape, staple the outside back fabric under the piping (see Techniques: Back Tack Tape) (T). Add one layer of polyester wadding over the calico and pull the fabric back over. At the underside of the sofa, fold the fabric under and staple it from the middle along the underside edge towards the sides. Folding the fabric under as you go, start to skewer along the frame line down each side until you reach the bottom edge, then complete stapling to the underside.

41 Finally, sew all pinned edges using slip stitch (see Techniques: Knots and Stitches).

T

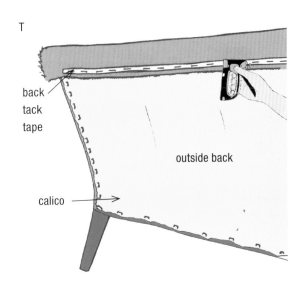

back
tack
tape

outside back

calico

TECHNIQUES

In this section you will find illustrated step-by-step guides to all the techniques I've used to make the ten featured projects, and, for those of you who want to progress to take on even more upholstery challenges, I have also included a couple of additional techniques that you may find useful when taking apart a chair or sofa, such as webbing a seat and using tack roll.

Techniques for Every Stage

It's not certain what you will find when you take a chair back to its frame. If more than a little sanding and re-varnishing is required, I'll show you how to strip and fill the frame so you can attach the layers securely.

Once you start to put the chair back together you may need to add webbing to a seat to create a platform for your materials or to create a sturdy backing for an arm, and I'll show you the correct way to use a web stretcher.

I'll introduce you to the knot all upholsterers need to know – the slip knot, as well as featuring other stitches which are used regularly in upholstery. How to measure and cut fabric is always a daunting task. I'll give you a starting point to work from. The use of back tack tape, forming cuts and making pleats to your fabric are also demonstrated.

Finally I'll take you through a few finishing techniques, including how to make a comfortable foam cushion, making trims such as piping and buttons, and sewing in a zip.

Understanding the Upholstery Process

One of the things you will start to notice as you gain a bit more experience is exactly how to layer a chair. Recognizing this will allow you to apply it to other items of furniture. I'll introduce you to the layers in modern upholstery. These are directly relevant to the projects in this book, but can be applied to other items of furniture too.

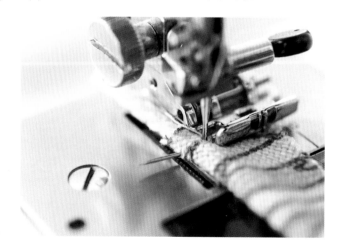

STRIPPING AND FILLING

When you are stripping a chair you work from the last item that was put onto it. With a nursery chair, for example, start by taking off the platform (dust) cloth, outside arms and outside back, and continue backwards from there. It's surprising the time this can take; allow a good 3–6 hours for stripping a small chair. You need to take out every single staple or tack so that the frame is completely bare; and if there are deep holes left in the frame by the tacks, these will need to be filled.

YOU WILL NEED

For stripping

Tack remover
Staple remover
Wooden mallet
Pliers

For filling

Bowl
Knife or wooden spatula
PVA glue
Smooth sawdust

Removing Tacks and Staples

For removing tacks you'll need a wooden mallet and a tack remover tool. For removing staples, swap the tack remover for a flat-ended staple remover and grab a pair pliers. Use the mallet to sharply hit the end of the tack or staple remover handle to thrust the blade underneath the tack or staple and lever them up (A) (B). Tacks should come right out but you might need the pliers to remove stubborn staples (C).

Filling the Frame

If tacks have left deep holes in the frame, you will need to fill them. This is a simple process using a home-made wood filler, made from one part PVA glue and two parts smooth sawdust (the sawdust should have no big splinters in it) (A). Mix the filler in small batches as a little goes a long way (B). Use a knife or wooden spatula to spread the filler into the holes and leave to dry (C).

LAYERS IN UPHOLSTERY

Using modern upholstery techniques for your projects means many of the fillings and edgings are pre-manufactured – this makes the process both simpler and quicker than with other upholstery techniques. Here I demonstrate how the layering of the furniture for the projects featured in this book has generally been worked. The simple reference diagram will help you to see what materials you start with and how the upholstery forms, layering up to top fabric.

Layering Pattern

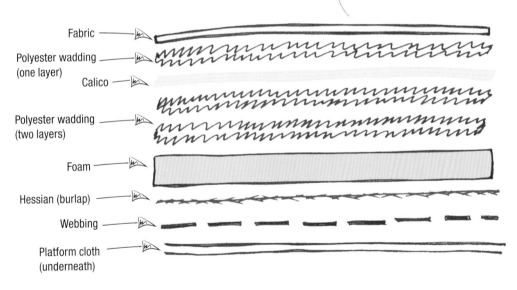

Fabric

Polyester wadding (one layer)

Calico

Polyester wadding (two layers)

Foam

Hessian (burlap)

Webbing

Platform cloth (underneath)

Your piece of furniture will contain many layers, from a webbed base to a wooden platform, tension springs or a spring mesh unit. Calico is used to hold all the layers together, acting as a fire-retardant barrier, whilst polyester wadding softens the hardness of the foam, and hessian creates a taut platform from which to start layering your stuffing. In between these layers, there will be hand sewing, spray glue and staples applied.

You are not always going to find this layering method in every chair, but this will produce a well upholstered and comfortable piece of furniture and is appropriate for the pieces I have chosen in this beginner's guide.

WEBBING AND TACK ROLL

The taut webbing created by the web stretcher increases strength in the back and arms of a chair and creates a solid seat base. I have used webbing only for the back or arms of the chair projects (the seats have been supported in other ways), but it is likely that you will need to know how to attach webbing to a seat, so I have included instructions. I have also included how to use tack roll as it is commonly used in modern upholstery to edge arms and seats even though I have not used it for any of the projects here.

YOU WILL NEED

Chalk
Jute webbing
Scissors
Staple gun
Staples, 10mm (⅜in) (minimum)
Tape measure
Web stretcher

Tip

Webbing comes in different strengths and thicknesses. I have used 5cm (2in) jute webbing for the projects.

Threading a Web Stretcher

Whether you are attaching webbing to an arm or to a seat, the method is the same. Start by stapling the webbing to one side of the frame, then use the web stretcher to pull it tight and staple it to the other side. Follow these instructions for threading the web stretcher.

1 Hold the web stretcher handle up to your chin with the groove towards you and the flat side away from you.

2 With the webbing roll attached to one side of the chair, pull it across the furniture and create a loop.

3 Take the loop of webbing through the hole of the web stretcher (groove side) and catch it with the dowel from the flat side. Adjust the tightness of the webbing by pulling the webbing and twisting the dowel.

4 With the groove, lever off the bottom edge of the furniture, pulling the webbing down so it is nice and tight, then secure the webbing in place with staples. I use 10mm (⅜in) staples, but you can use longer s hafts if your staple gun will allow.

webbing direction

dowel

web stretcher groove

Placement of Webbing

If you are webbing the inside back of an armchair, generally for foam stuffing, it will take 2–4 pieces of webbing. These are usually applied vertically and attached to a rail bar at the bottom of the frame (**A**). How many webbing strips you apply will depend on how wide the back is, so work out how many you need and try to get them evenly spaced. If no back rail exists, create one by applying a strip of webbing horizontally across the bottom of the frame, leaving a gap for fabric to be tucked under. If an arm rail is not present beneath the arm rest, then one strip of webbing applied horizontally from the inside front of the arm to the back (**B**) should suffice.

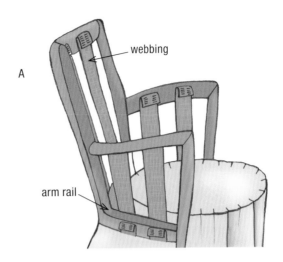

Webbing an Arm

1 Use chalk to mark out where to place the webbing onto the inside of the arm frame.

2 Keeping the webbing on the roll, place the end of the webbing onto one side of the frame where you have marked. Allowing for a 5cm (2in) overhang for a turning allowance, staple the webbing in place (**A**) with three rows of staples, four to five staples in each row. (Do not staple it too close to the edge of the frame as there are lots more layers to be stapled on yet.) (**B**)

3 Fold the end of the webbing over and staple two more rows, making sure they are placed in between the previously stapled rows.

4 Take the webbing roll across to the other side of the arm where marked and thread the webbing through the web stretcher and lever off the frame holding it taut (if it starts to creak, it's probably being pulled too tight). Staple in place, as before (**C**).

5 Cut the webbing from the roll leaving a 5cm (2in) turning allowance. Fold the end of the webbing over and staple two rows, as before (**D**).

Webbing a Seat

1 Chalk out the placement of the webbing, starting from the mid point of each side (**A**). Depending on the size of the seat frame, three to four strips of webbing are usual, with a gap of around 5cm (2in) in between each piece.

2 To apply the webbing, see Webbing an Arm for the basic method. Start by stapling the first webbing strip to the middle of the back of the frame (**B**), using the web stretcher to attach the webbing to the front of the chair. Attach the remaining vertical strips.

3 To apply the webbing horizontally across the frame, weave the first (middle) piece in and out of the vertical strips, remembering to keep the webbing on the roll (**C**). Staple in place on one side, pull with the web stretcher, staple and cut from the roll.

4 Weave the horizontal webbing strip in the opposite direction, above or below the middle piece. Continue until all the webbing has been applied (**D**).

Using Tack Roll

Although I have not used tack roll for the upholstery projects in this book, it is worth a mention as it is often used in modern upholstery around a seat edge or arm edge to build up the height up and contain the stuffing. Tack roll is applied after the webbing and a layer of hessian is attached. The desired length is cut, taking into consideration any legs or arms. Staple in place with 10mm (⅜in), or larger, staples around the edge of the seat (**A**). The foam will then be added within and on top of the completed edge roll (**B**).

KNOTS AND STITCHES

The upholstery knot, or slip knot, is the first thing any upholsterer will learn: it is used on each one of my projects, be it at the start of the upholstery process to tie in hessian, or at the end when sewing the fabric onto the outside of a chair. Other hand-sewing stitches are also covered.

YOU WILL NEED

Appropriate thread (upholstery twine, button twine, upholstery thread)
Appropriate needle (curved needle, half-curved needle, small sewing needle)

Upholstery Knot (Slip Knot)

The upholstery knot not only draws two pieces of fabric together, but it also allows you to loosen or tighten, which is particularly helpful when tying in buttons. You can either wrap it once or twice for extra strength.

1 Single thread the needle and stitch it through the fabric; remove needle.

2 Holding the long end of thread in one hand and the short end in the other (**A**), take the short end and wrap it over the long end catching two fingers in the loop, and continuing to take it around the back of the long end (**B**).

3 Pull the thread around your fingers again and around the back of the long end to create a double loop (**C**). Pull your fingers out of the double loop and pinch it together (**D**).

4 Take the short end, pop it through the loop (**E**) and pull it tight. Pull the long end to draw the knot up towards the fabric (**F**).

create loop around fingers

long end

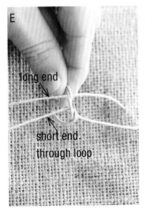
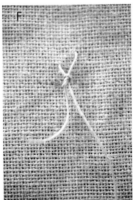

long end

short end through loop

Tip

Wrapping the thread around your finger as you stitch helps to create an easier loop for the slip knot.

Slip Stitch

Slip stitch pulls two pieces of fabric together, hiding the stitches beneath for an invisible seam, so it is often used for finishing touches. It is best achieved with a curved needle.

1 Fold the turning allowance on the top fabric and pin it along the single piping edge butting it right up against the piping (**A**).

2 Attach the thread with an upholstery knot at the top edge of the piping. Stitch a small running stitch into the fold of the turning allowance of your top fabric only (**B**) and pull taut.

3 Take the curved needle back through the piping edge, tight to the piping. The piping should be stitched at the exact point where the needle leaves the top fabric (**C**) so that when pulled tight the stitches align and are invisible (**D**).

4 Continue going back and forth through the piping and top fabric with small stitches no more than 1cm (⅜in) apart. Remove the pins before each stitch and pull the top fabric and piping together so they are taut after each stitch (**E**). When you reach the bottom, take the stitch through the piping a couple of times and catch the loop pulling tight to secure the thread. Snip the thread and push the end behind the fabric.

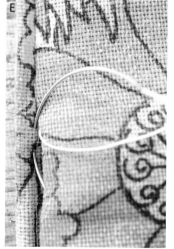

Tip

A smaller curved needle is recommended for sewing up edges to ensure the stitches are not made too far apart.

Tip

This step-by-step assumes you are applying fabric to a piped edge, but the same technique can be applied to an edge without piping – just follow the line of the chair frame for accurate placement.

Blanket Stitch

This stitch is useful for stitching materials to metal edges. It is used around spring mesh units to hold hessian in place, keeping it taut to the curve of the frame where stapling is not possible.

1 Start with an upholstery knot, tying it around the frame and pulling it tight (**A**). Stitch the twine at 1cm (⅜in) intervals, about 1cm (⅜in) from the edge. Enter the twine from the top and exit from the bottom. As the twine exits the hessian, pop the needle through the loop and pull taut (**B**).

2 Continue around the edge (**C**) until you reach the end. Finish with a double stitch, catching the thread through the loop.

OTHER STITCHES AND KNOTS

There are plenty of other stitches and knots used in upholstery hand stitching. Here are a few more I have used for the projects included in this book.

Running Stitch

Running stitch is worked by passing the needle in and out of the fabric. The longer stitch is visible from the top side. Start with an upholstery knot.

Herringbone Stitch

This stitch is used to sew the two stretchy hems of stockinette together on a foam cushion and can be sewn right to left or left to right. Starting with an upholstery knot on the bottom hem, bring your needle diagonally across to the top hem, take a small running stitch from left to right, then bring your needle diagonally back to the bottom hem and take a small running stitch from right to left. Continue all the way along the hem. Finish with a double stitch, catching the thread through the loop.

The Cow Hitch

This knot produces a strong hold onto a spring, making the cord less likely to unravel. Wrap the cord around the spring, as if tying in a figure of '8', then pop the cord end through the bottom loop and pull tight.

BACK TACK TAPE

Back tack tape (cardboard tack strip) allows you to staple fabric to an edge without the need for hand sewing. It is only used on top fabric and provides a seamless straight edge. Although unsuitable for curved areas, it can be applied to a slight curve by making a few release cuts in the tape. Use it on the top or side edges of the outside areas of a chair such as the arms and the back.

YOU WILL NEED

Back tack tape (cardboard tack strip)
Fabric
56g (2oz) polyester wadding
Scissors
Staples (long shaft such as 10mm/⅜in)
Staple gun

Applying Back Tack Tape

1 Back tack tape can be applied on its own or up to the edge of piping. If using piping, start by adding the piping along the edge, stapling it in place.

2 Place the **top edge** of your fabric **wrong side** facing up to sit in the seam allowance of the piping (usually 1.5cm/⅝in) (**A**).

3 Cut your back tack tape to fit. Lay the back tack tape butting it up to the piping line (or the edge if not using piping). Hold the tape with one hand and start to staple along it holding the staple gun in your other hand, using a long shaft staple such as a 10mm (⅜in) staple (**B**): it helps to put a holding staple in the middle of the tape first.

4 Place one layer of polyester wadding (batting) over the back tack tape (**C**), then fold your fabric back over to lie on top of the wadding with the **right side** facing up (**D**). You can now continue to staple the fabric in place as required, depending on the project.

Tip

Back tack tape is also useful where a tidy folded edge is needed, such as on the top edge of a base of a blanket box where the fabric sits under a lid.

MEASURING AND CUTTING FABRIC

Before stripping your piece of furniture, your first job is to measure it up for your fabric requirements. It is best to measure from the existing upholstery as this gives you a guide to the extra allowance required for the upholstery layers. Once you have taken accurate measurements, the simplest way to determine how much fabric you will need is to draw up a cutting plan for your fabric. This will be your guide to cutting out your fabric. Using the patchwork nursery chair as an example, I will guide you through these important stages.

Measuring up for the patchwork nursery chair below.

Measuring Up

To measure a chair, you need to break it up into sections to represent each piece of fabric you will need to cut. As an example, I have broken down the patchwork nursery chair into sections as shown in the diagram. In addition, you will need to measure for piping and any loose box cushions.

Make a list of the sections of your piece of furniture and write the measurements of the length and width of each section. When measuring make sure you push your tape measure right into the crevices and add extra for turning allowance. I start with the inside sections, Inside Back (IB), Inside Arms (IA) and Seat (S), and as the fabric length has to reach the bottom of the frame and be attached to the outside areas, I add an extra 10cm (4in). The outside sections, Seat Front (SF), Outside Arms (OA) and Outside Back (OB) can be allocated a smaller turning allowance as these sections will be folded under and hand sewn in most instances, so I usually allow 1.5cm (⅝in) at the edges.

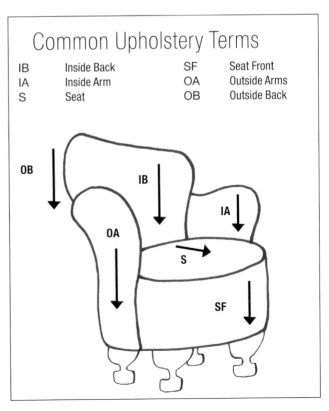

Common Upholstery Terms

IB	Inside Back	SF	Seat Front
IA	Inside Arm	OA	Outside Arms
S	Seat	OB	Outside Back

Creating a Cutting Plan

A cutting plan is a paper representation of the width and length of your fabric requirements. Basically you are marking up an imaginary piece of fabric before you cut it. The cutting plan does not need to be made to scale necessarily, but I find marking mine in measures of 1m (1yd) going down the page can sometimes help with a complicated pattern repeat. I always make sure to mark the width too, and this is particularly useful when working with narrower vintage fabrics. As an example, I've created a cutting plan for the patchwork nursery chair for a plain fabric with a standard working width of 137cm (54in) with the measurements taken noted on each section. The cutting plan will vary from chair to chair, and, if you are working with patterned rather than plain fabric, there are other factors to take into consideration.

Plain Fabric Cutting Plan

Start with the largest sections of the chair and arrange them on the plan, then fit the smaller sections in around the larger sections. Apply the measurements just as rectangles at this stage as it is easier to place them onto the plan. Be sure to make a note of the direction of the warp and weft threads in your fabric and make sure you cut in line with this.

Patterned Fabric Cutting Plan

For patterned fabrics, the pattern repeat needs to be added to the cutting plan, and you will need more fabric for a chair made from patterned fabric. I like to draw a little dot on the paper where the pattern starts from and draw a mid point as a dashed line down the paper (see diagram, Considerations for Patterned Fabric). To reduce waste in your fabric, try and get the pattern mid-point width close to the selvedge and work down the larger sections from there if you can. Whichever way you cut a patterned fabric, it's important to find a centre line for your pattern from the start and to stick to it.

Cutting Your Fabric

Roll the fabric out flat. It's best to cut from the face of the fabric for accuracy, particularly if you have a pattern. (When you buy a roll of fabric, the face is the inside of the roll and is usually marked with a little sticker from the manufacturer.) For large pieces of furniture, like the mid-century sofa, it's advisable to cut all the fabric at once. Using sharp sewing scissors, start by cutting your fabric as marked out in your fabric cutting plan. As you cut each piece, pin a paper note to it to mark which direction is top and what section of the chair it is for.

Cutting Plan
This cutting plan is for the patchwork nursery chair for a plain fabric with a standard working width of 137cm (54in).

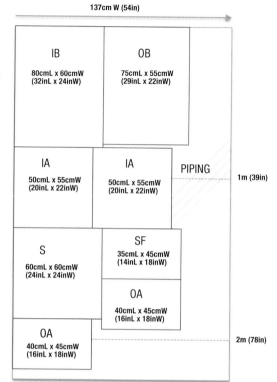

Warp and Weft Threads

Warp Vertical threads that run along the length of the fabric.

Weft Horizontal threads that run from selvedge to selvedge (side to side).

Note: non-woven fabrics such as leather, suede, felt, vinyl and knits do not have warp and weft threads.

Considerations for Patterned Fabric

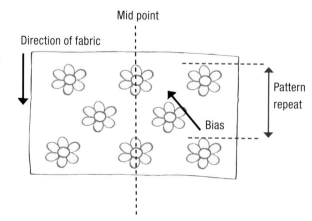

FABRIC CUTS AND PLEATS

Generally, a fabric cut is made whenever your fabric comes into contact with a pointy part of the furniture frame, such as a leg, or where it has to tuck around a corner. If the fabric looks misaligned or wrinkled, a cut may be required. The upholstery of most chairs will require either the 'V' cut or the straight cut, and perfecting a tight bed sheet pleat at the corners of your furniture can really make a difference to the finished look.

YOU WILL NEED

Skewers
Small sharp scissors
Staple gun and staples

Fabric Cuts: 'V' Cut

This cut is made when your fabric hits a flat surface and where the fabric has to fold around three sides, on a chair leg for example. I have demonstrated the cutting of a 'V' cut on calico, but the process is the same whether you're working on hessian, platform cloth or top fabric.

1 Feel with your fingers where the fabric hits the chair frame and place a skewer to mark the exact point at each of the edges (**A**).

2 The fold is formed by cutting a straight line towards the middle of the leg (or flat surface) and then going diagonally towards each skewer point as marked in the photo for guidance (**B**).

3 Remove the skewers from the fabric. Fold the middle triangle and sides to fit neatly around the frame (**C**). Staple the fabric down.

Tip

Practise makes perfect, so practise with the calico as much as you like before adding the top fabric.

A

B

C

Tip

When cutting the release cuts on your top fabric snip a little slower. Different fabrics fray to different extents, and if you have a thick weave fabric the cut can travel a little further.

Fabric Cuts: Straight Cut

A straight cut is generally made into a corner, when a leg is angled or only one or two sides need folding around the frame. This cut is also used to fold fabric from the seat underneath the frame of the chair.

1 Find the point where you want your cut to end. Fold the fabric back towards you. Skewer the point at which the fabric fold hits the frame (**A**).

A

Tip

If you want a practise run before cutting your top fabric, pop a piece of scrap calico over your top fabric before you make the cut.

2 The line is either cut diagonally or straight towards the skewer point, depending on how much turning allowance you need (**B**) (**C**).

B

C

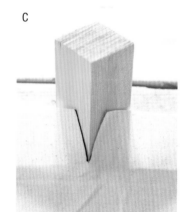

3 Pull out the skewer and fold back each side (**D**). Staple your fabric in place.

D

Bed Sheet Pleat

The fold of a bed sheet pleat should be invisible from the front of the chair or footstool, being visible from the side only. Bulky and misaligned pleats can result from trying to tuck under too much fabric, so I'll show you how to cut the bulk out.

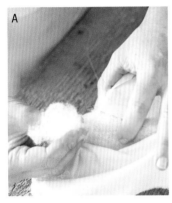

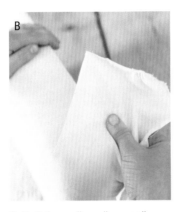

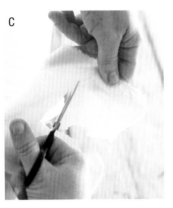

1 At the corner of the piece you are pleating, start by removing some of the wadding underneath the calico; pinch the wadding together and tear a little bit off (**A**).

2 Pull the calico diagonally towards the corner on the side you want to pleat over and create a fold (**B**).

3 To reduce bulk, cut a square from the corner about 2.5cm (1in) from the folded edge and 2.5cm (1in) from the corner of the base (**C**).

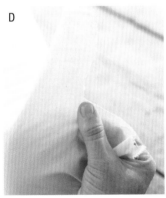

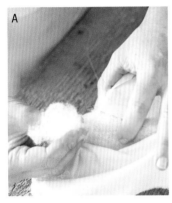

4 Pull the fabric tight into the corner as before (**D**) and staple underneath the base (**E**).

5 Pleat the folded calico over to the corner edge, pulling the fabric taut underneath the pleat (**F**).

6 Now pull the pleat tight and attach to the underside of the base with staples (**G**).

BUTTONS

Fabric-covered buttons are a lovely way to bring some individuality to your furniture. There are several ways to cover buttons: I often use a button-making machine at my local upholstery store, but these machines are expensive to buy. Alternatively, haberdashery stores sell kits, however I have found that these don't work so well with thick upholstery fabrics. Here I show you how to make your own fabric-covered buttons and how to attach them to your furniture. This method is particularly suitable for larger button backs, when small quantities are required.

YOU WILL NEED

For making buttons:
Fabric
Cotton thread
Button twine
Large button back
Hand sewing needle
Polyester wadding
Scissors

For attaching buttons:
Fabric-covered button with button
    twine
Staple gun
8mm (⁵⁄₁₆in) staples
Small scrap piece of calico
Button needle

Making Buttons

1 Take your button back, place it onto your fabric and mark an area roughly half as big again. (I drew around a ramekin jar to get the circular shape.) The circle should be sized to enable you to fold edges into the middle of the button without them touching. Cut the circle out (**A**).

2 Working on the wrong side of the fabric circle, make an upholstery knot about 5mm (¼in) from the edge and sew a small running stitch all the way around the edge of the circle (**B**) to meet the knot again. Do not unthread the needle.

Tip

Use pretty vintage barkcloth fabrics and centre the pattern in the middle of the button.

3 Take the button back and thread it with sufficient button twine to pull through your furniture – about 50cm (20in) – making sure the ends are equal length (**C**). If you are using a button with a loop shaft, you won't have to thread the button twine at step 3.

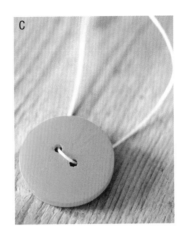

4 Cut a couple of pieces of polyester wadding to fit perfectly over the top of the button. Place the button and wadding into the fabric circle and hold in place with the finger of one hand, while pulling the running stitch thread taut with the other hand (**D**) to cinch in the back.

5 Turn the button over to check that it is nicely centred, adjusting if necessary. Overlock the thread several times into the back to secure it (**E**), making sure not to cross over the button twine, which needs to remain free. The finished button should have two pieces of button twine hanging out of the back for attaching to the furniture (**F**).

Attaching Your Button

1 Mark the buttonhole position on the top fabric with a skewer. Thread both ends of your button twine through the button needle and push the needle through exactly where the skewer is positioned to come out at the hole (**A**).

2 Roll a little bit of scrap calico between the lengths of button twine and place it over the hole. Tie an upholstery knot over the scrap calico with the ends of the twine and pull taut (**B**).

3 Staple the twine in a zigzag formation using 8mm (⁵⁄₁₆in) staples. This ensures the button won't pop out of position (**C**).

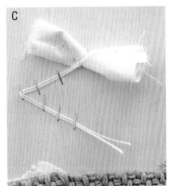

SINGLE AND DOUBLE PIPING

Piping is used as a decorative edging in upholstery, shaping and silhouetting the furniture frame. Single piping is generally added around the top back edge, arm frames and cushion edges, and it is usually sewn in by machine or by hand. Double piping is used in the same way as braiding or decorative tacks, around the seating, arm pads or bottom edge of a seat frame, and it is either glued in place with hot glue or tacked with gimp pins.

YOU WILL NEED

For making piping:
Chalk and metre/yard ruler
Sewing machine and zip foot or
    piping foot
Fabric
Piping cord
Cotton thread
Scissors

For applying piping:
Staple gun and staples or sewing
    machine (single piping)
Hot glue gun or gimp pins (double
    piping)

Tip
Fabric for piping can be cut on the straight or on the bias. If you have a strict pattern to match, cut on the straight.

Single Piping

1 Place the piping cord into the middle of your fabric strip; roll the fabric over so its edges meet with about 1cm (⅜in) of the cord showing and pin at the top (**A**). If you are taking the piping cord from a roll (cob), then leave this attached to the roll to ensure you don't under cut the cord.

2 Place the top of the wrapped piping under a zip or piping foot and lower the needle into the fabric to hold it in place. Slowly start to sew in a straight line as close to the cord as possible (**B**) continuing until you reach the end.

3 The finished single piping (**C**) is either stapled or sewn in place. To apply it to a front scroll arm, it is best to sew it onto the fabric and pull it over the arm for a neat finish; to attach it around a corner edge, snip some release cuts into the piping selvedge.

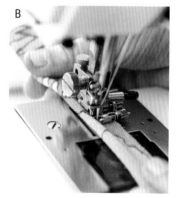

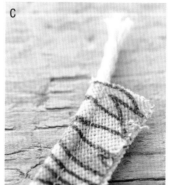

Tip
One metre (39in) of standard width fabric cut on the bias yields 25m (27yd) of piping.

Double Piping

1 Place your desired cut length of cord about a third of the way across the fabric strip. Fold the left side of the fabric across over the cord and hold in place with your fingers (**A**). Lay the second piece of piping cord next to the first, on top of the folded over fabric (**B**). Pull the right side of the fabric over both pieces of cord, turn the whole thing over, and pin in place from behind (**C**).

2 Adjust the needle into the middle eye of the zip foot and sew directly down the middle of the double piping. Hold it in place as you sew and continually stop to adjust the piping and fabric to make sure you have a tight roll over the two bits of piping until you reach the end (**D**).

3 Trim the unwanted fabric from the back of the double piping (**E**). Attach the double piping with hot glue or gimp pins. If you have a show edge, take the bulk of the piping out of the end leaving some fabric to fold under. Glue this first, then glue the back to the edge of the chair.

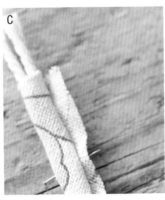

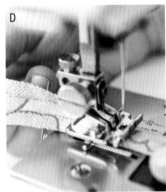

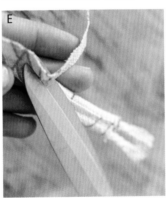

Cutting and Joining

Use a metre ruler (yardstick) to chalk a line diagonally across your fabric at a 45-degree angle. Chalk another line 4cm (1½in) above or below (**A**). Continue until you have enough strips to make the desired piping length, adding a 1.5cm (⅝in) seam allowance at each end. Join two cut strips neatly by placing one on top of the other, right side to wrong side and cut a 45-degree angle across the top. Turn the strips right sides together and place one on top of the other, aligning the angled edges for a teepee-shaped triangle (**B**). Pin together and straight stitch. Cut off any excess close to join line.

MAKING UP A FOAM CUSHION

If you are getting a new set of foam cushion inners for your box cushions, you can make them a little more comfortable by adding a couple of layers of polyester wadding (batting) covered with stockinette. Not only will your cushions be spongier, but the stockinette layer will make it easier to get the cushion cover on and off for laundering or making adjustments. The overall look is definitely more aesthetically pleasing and it certainly makes the cushions comfier to sit on. Whatever the shape of your foam cushion, this process fits all.

YOU WILL NEED

Foam cushion inner
56g (2oz) polyester wadding (batting)
Stockinette
Upholstery cotton thread
Needle: large curved, half curved or large straight
Skewers
Scissors

Tip
A stockinette cover avoids the clingy static you sometimes get when fabric and foam come into contact.

Preparing a Foam Cushion for Top Fabric Covering

1 Cover the whole of the foam cushion, including sides, with two layers of polyester wadding (batting) (**A**). (Some people spray glue the wadding in place, but I don't find I need to as it usually sticks on its own.)

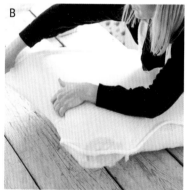

2 Next stretch the stockinette across the top of the cushion to see how much to cut. Carefully feed the cushion through the cut stockinette so that the open edges are at the cushion sides and **not** at the front or back edge of the cushion. Start with the stockinette rolled in the middle of the cushion and tease out with your hands as this will eliminate the chance of pulls (**B**).

3 Starting from the middle, bring the open sides of the stockinette together; roll to create a folded seam and pin with a skewer (**C**). Continue along the edge until you have three or four skewers in place. Turn the cushion to the other edge and skewer along the opposite side, again starting from the middle (**D**). If necessary, trim the stockinette if it is too bulky – you don't want it showing through the fabric.

4 At the ends, fold the stockinette inwards and skewer (**E**). Once both sides have been fully pinned, you are ready to hand sew them closed.

5 Using a curved needle and upholstery thread or carpet thread, tie an upholstery knot at the first skewer (see Techniques: Knots and Stitches) (**F**).

6 Sew herringbone stitch along the edges to seam the stockinette: this creates a zigzag line of straight stitches that overlap to bring the edges together tightly with reduced bulk (see Techniques: Knots and Stitches) (**G**). Remove the skewers as you go and at the end tie your stitch off taking it through the stockinette a few times and, catching a loop, pulling it taut (**H**).

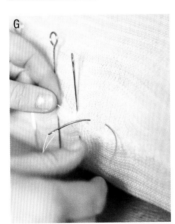

Tip

If you prefer, you can pay your foam supplier to add a wadding/stockinette layer for you.

PUTTING IN A ZIP

This simple method for putting in a zip can be used for box cushions or decorative cushions. If you can, buy a few metres of zip from a roll as this will enable you to adapt the zip length according to what you are making. Zip roll comes with separate zip heads that you add manually, and it can be bought in dark or light tones to match your top fabric, as can the zip heads. To attach the zip to the fabric use a zip foot or a piping foot on your sewing machine.

YOU WILL NEED

Zip

Zip head

Sewing machine and zip foot or
   piping foot

Pinking shears

Upholstery thread

Small dress pins

Quick unpick

Ironing board and iron

Putting in a Zip

A zip can be attached to the bottom edge of the border or in the middle of the border. The method described below adds a zip to the middle, but if you want to attach it to the bottom, just use the back edge of the bottom side of the cushion and the bottom edge of the border and attach in the same way.

1 First you need to join the two matching border pieces of top fabric with right sides together. For plain fabrics, place right sides together and sew a seam 1.5cm (⅝in) from the edge. If you have a pattern to match, place one of the pieces of fabric on your work table right side up. Take the other piece, fold its top edge to a 1.5cm (⅝in) turning allowance, and match the pattern to the first piece. To secure, pin lengthways under the fold (on the wrong side) (**A**) and sew (**B**). Once the seam is sewn and the fabric folded back and pressed, your pattern should be perfectly matched (**C**).

A

B

C

2 Trim the seam edges with pinking shears to reduce fraying (**D**), or finish the seam edges with zigzag stitch if your fabric is particularly prone to fraying. On the fabric wrong side press the seam open (**E**).

3 Cut the zip slightly longer than the border and place it face down onto the pressed seam and pin in place (**F**). Turn the border to the right side and sew down one edge with straight stitch using a zipper or piping foot. The sew line should be as close to the seam as you can get it (**G**). Turn the border to the wrong side.

4 Now add the zip head: at the zip head end of the zip, snip a 45-degree angle on one side of the tape towards the teeth. Pull the zip head with its back facing you onto the unsnipped side and pull down pinching the snipped side inwards to catch the zip head (**H**). This may take a few attempts.

5 Turn the border right side to sew the other edge from the opposite end to the attached zip head; this will allow you to pull the zip down into the sewn area to continue sewing in a straight line (**I**).

6 With a quick unpick, open the seam inbetween your stitching lines on the right side (**J**), leaving a seam allowance at each end of the zip (**K**).

GLOSSARY

Back Tack Tape (Cardboard Tack Strip)
A length of cardboard used to join a piece of fabric to a piece of furniture creating a straight edge and eliminating the need to stitch.

Bayonet Needle (Square Point Needle) A double ended needle that has a square tip point. The needle can slide through hessian and other layers with ease.

Bias A diagonal cut which is a 45- degree angle across the grain of a fabric.

Button Needle This is a straight needle with either a single point or a double point. They range in length.

Calico A 100% cotton fabric used as a lining in modern and traditional upholstery. It can be made fire retardant.

Curved Needles Available in varying sizes, curved needles are used for joining fabrics in upholstery and stitching twine, amongst other uses.

Hessian (Burlap) A strong coarse fabric made from hemp or jute that comes in different weights. It is used to cover over springs, as a platform cloth, or as a layer over stuffing in traditional upholstery.

Inside Arm When a chair is broken into sections for measuring and cutting fabric, the inside arm refers to the inside part of the arm.

Inside Back When a chair is broken into sections for measuring and cutting fabric, the inside back refers to the inside part of the back that you rest your back against.

Laid (Lacing) Cord A strong string made from hemp or flax. The cord has no stretch which makes it perfect for tying (lashing) springs.

Outside Arm When a chair is broken into sections for measuring and cutting fabric, the outside arm refers to the outside part of the arm.

Outside Back When a chair is broken into sections for measuring and cutting fabric, the outside back refers to the outside back part of the chair.

Pattern Matching The act of fitting fabric onto a chair to make it form a pattern match and flow down the chair correctly. Pattern matching is determined by the measuring and cutting of a fabric.

Piping Cord (Welt Cord) A smooth cord made from cotton strands. It comes either pre-shrunk, covered in a fine stockinette, bleached or unbleached, and is available in various thicknesses, usually offered as thin, medium or thick.

Platform Cloth (Dust Cover or Bottoming Cloth) This is usually a strong black cotton fabric that is stapled or tacked to the underside of the chair. It is also used under seat cushions as a barrier over tension springs.

Polyester Wadding (Dacron) A soft polyester fibre that is used to pad foam seating in modern upholstery. It comes in different weights starting from 56g (2oz).

PVA Glue A white water-based adhesive that is ready mixed and dries clear.

Railroading Fabric is usually cut with the fabric going up the roll. A railroaded fabric is turned to have the pattern go across the roll.

Regulator A long thin tool with a flat-edged top that is useful to adjust fillings and to help with folds.

Selvedge The edge of a fabric, often self finished to prevent unravelling or fraying.

Skewers A holding pin for temporary fixing of materials. Normally 75mm-100mm (3-4 in) in length.

Spring Mesh Unit A complete set of springs that fit inside a seat frame and attach to the frame. The bottom of the spring is fixed to metal bars, whilst the top of the spring is attached to a wire mesh that forms the platform for the seat stuffing.

Staple Remover A hand-held tool with a flat head to lift staples from a frame when stripping down a frame. It is used in conjunction with a wooden mallet.

Tack Hammer A small hand-held hammer used for hitting tacks into a chair frame. It has a magnetic end to hit the tack in place before hammering.

Tack Remover A hand-held tool with a V-shaped head, used alongside a mallet.

Tack Roll (Edge Roll) A foam or paper roll sometimes used in modern upholstery to hold foam pads onto a seat, to avoid foam creeping over the front edge of the seat.

Tension Springs Stretched coiled plastic or cloth-covered springs used on seats and seat backs. They are usually hooked onto a plate on the frame.

Twine, Button This is a strong nylon twine used for tying in buttons. It does not rot and is abrasion resistant.

Twine, Cord This is a high quality linen thread with a tight twist. It's used to tie in stuffing in upholstery. It is available in several different weights.

Warp In weaving of the cloth, the warp is a set of vertical threads that run lengthways.

Weft The weft is a set of horizontal threads that are woven between the warp threads.

ABOUT THE AUTHOR

Vicky Grubb is an upholsterer, self-confessed vintage-fabric hoarder and mum to two little tinkers. Working out of The Upholstery Studio, based in Bournemouth on the south coast of England, Vicky takes commissions and teaches her one-day and six-week workshops, as well as working on her own furniture creations and writing a textile and upholstery blog. She, her vintage fabrics and her furniture have featured in magazines, including *Homes and Antiques* and *Red*.

www.theupholsterycabin.co.uk

AUTHOR'S ACKNOWLEDGEMENTS

First and foremost I would like to thank my family, particularly my super duper husband who encourages and reassures me every day. Also, thanks too to my patient boys, who have had to put up with mummy being distracted and talking non stop about 'the boring book' for months; and to my lovely Mum who has taken the kiddies on many occasions to allow me to upholster into the night.

I am so grateful to my publisher Ame, for her continuing support throughout the process and for always being there for me; for their help and advice, Charly, Emma, Honor and Cheryl; for some fabulous pictures, Jack at Bang Wallop. Also, special thanks to Sam, my talented illustrator, who had to put up with a lot of to-ing and fro-ing, but who was always patient and understanding.

Without the talent and patience of my upholstery teacher Sarah Bolton and the thousands of photocopied handouts she provided throughout my learning, and my diploma classmates who brought the laughs to our weekly upholstery class, I am sure I wouldn't have written this book.

I would like to give special thanks for all the momentous things people of all experience are doing with upholstery, from my keen and enthusiastic students, to the creations on Facebook forums such as 'the upholsterers friendly forum' and 'the upholstery club' that continue to inspire me every day; equally, to those upholsterers from around the world on Instagram - keep posting those pictures! #upholstery

SUPPLIERS

Upholstery Suppliers

(UK) F C Hancox Upholstery Supplies Ltd (fchancoxfoam.co.uk)
(USA) DIY Upholstery Supply LLC (diyupholsterysupply.com)
(USA) Philmore Upholstery Supply (upholsterysuppliesandfoam.com)
(NZ) Furniture Components (furnco.co.nz)

Trims & Haberdashery

(UK) Bournemouth Upholstery Centre (bourneupholstery.co.uk)
(UK) Ringwood Fabrics (ringwoodfabrics.co.uk)
(USA) Mood Fabrics (moodfabrics.com)

Project Fabric Suppliers

Laundry Bin Vintage towelling fabric from Something Fine (somethingfine.co.uk).
Fabric Focus, left to right: Swan Lake by Bengt & Lotta (bengt-lotta.se); Dragonfly, Colour Heaven by Expression (cmltd.co.uk); Trumpet/Flowers/Emerald, by Amy Butler (amybutlerdesign.com).

Danish-style Dining Chair Aldgate East Major by Lucy Rainbow (Flock.org.uk).
Fabric Focus, left to right: Pug Linen by Fenella Smith (fenellasmith.co.uk); Ratten by Scion (scion.uk.com); Stowe Denim by Clarke & Clarke (clarke-clarke.co.uk).

Blanket Box Pretty Maids, Duck Egg by Vanessa Arbuthnott (vanessaarbuthnott.co.uk) and Angie Lewin, Stellar at St Judes (stjudesfabrics.co.uk).
Fabric Focus, left to right: Vintage novelty barkcloth fabric by Something Fine (somethingfine.co.uk); Dolce Midnight by Warwick Fabrics (warwick.co.uk); Rose Barkcloth by A Piece of Cloth (apiecefocloth.com.au).

Ercol Sofa Cava 3 by Kvadrat (kvadrat.dk), vintage tea towels from Pineapple Retro Bucket (pineappleretro.co.uk).
Fabric Focus left to right: Nettle Aztec Maya by Camira Fabrics (camirafabrics.com); Marylebone Kingfisher by Kirkby (kirbyfrdign.com); Troon by Bute Fabrics (butefabrics.com).

Vintage Sewing Box Vintage Dekoplus fabric from Jane Foster (janefoster.co.uk), vintage purple cotton lining from Something Fine (somethingfine.co.uk).
Fabric Focus, left to right: David Whitehead from Something Fine; Garden Birds by Cath Kidston (cathkidston.com); Dandelion by St Judes (stjudesfabrics.com).

Fluted Headboard Cirkelblomma by Hus and Hem (husandhem.co.uk).
Fabric Focus, left to right: Liason by Warwick Fabrics (warwick.co.uk); vintage fabric from Rainbow Vintage Home (rainbowvintagehome.co.uk); Highland Linen by Tinsmiths (tinsmiths.co.uk).

Round Bedroom Chair Grand Kyoto Koi by Korla (korlahome.com), purple cotton velvet from John Lewis (johnlewis.com).
Fabric Focus left to right: Haga by Spira (spirainredning.se); Wicker Linen by Fermoie (fermoie.com); Peony Velvet by Tinsmiths (tinsmiths.co.uk).

Buttoned Footstool Vintage barkcloth fabric from Something Fine (somethingfine.co.uk).
Fabric Focus, left to right: Clunie Burn by Isle Mill (Islemill.com); Rocco by Prestigious Textiles (prestigious.co.uk); Jardin-Boheme Cheree by Harlequin (harlequin.uk.com).

Patchwork Nursery Chair Vintage floral barkcloth fabric from Something Fine (somethingfine.co.uk).
Fabric Focus, left to right: London Scene by Cath Kidston (cathkidston.com); Romana Fuscia by Clarke & Clarke (clarke-clarke.co.uk); Ionian by Villa Nova (villanova.co.uk).

Mid-century Sofa Coda 2 by Kvadrat (kvadrat.dk). *Fabric Focus, left to right:* Kilmory by Bute Fabrics (butefabrics.com); Odissa by Jane Churchill (designs.colfax.com); Carnival by Jane Churchill (designs.colfax.com).

INDEX

A DAVID AND CHARLES BOOK
© David and Charles, Ltd 2015

David and Charles is an imprint of David and Charles, Ltd
Suite A, Tourism House, Pynes Hill, Exeter, EX2 5WS

Text, Designs and Videos © Vicky Grubb 2015
Layout, Photography and Artwork © David and Charles, Ltd 2015

First published in the UK and USA in 2015

A catalogue record for this book is available from the British Library.

ISBN-13: 978-1-4463-0532-4 UK paperback
ISBN-13: 978-1-44630605-5 US paperback
ISBN-13: 978-1-4463-7051-3 UK EPUB
ISBN-13: 978-1-4463-7280-7 US EPUB

Printed in the UK by Buxton Press for:
David and Charles, Ltd
Suite A, Tourism House, Pynes Hill, Exeter, EX2 5WS

10 9 8 7 6 5

Acquisitions Editor: Ame Verso
Desk Editor: Emma Gardner, Honor Head
Project Editor: Cheryl Brown
Designer: Charly Bailey
Photographer: Jack Kirby
Production Manager: Beverley Richardson

David and Charles publishes high-quality books on a wide range of subjects.
For more information visit www.davidandcharles.com.

Layout of the digital edition of this book may vary depending on reader hardware and display settings.